MORE BATHS LESS TALKING

MORE BATHS LESS TALKING

by

NICK HORNBY

BELIEVER BOOKS

a division of
McSWEENEY'S

BELIEVER BOOKS

a division of

McSWEENEY'S

849 Valencia Street
San Francisco, CA 94110

Copyright © 2012 Nick Hornby

These pieces appeared between May 2010 and
December 2011 in the *Believer* magazine.

www.believermag.com

Cover illustration by *Charles Burns!*

Printed in Canada by The Prolific Group.

ISBN: 978-1-938073-05-2

ALSO BY NICK HORNBY

For Harry Ritchie

CONTENTS

INTRODUCTION

This book is the fourth collection of award-winning English novelist, screenwriter, journalist, and critic Nick Hornby's monthly books column for the *Believer*. It covers the last two and a half years of Hornby's reading diary, which appears in the magazine under the title "Stuff I've Been Reading." The column always begins in the same way: Hornby lists the books he's bought that month, followed by the books he's actually read. The seasoned reader, accustomed to the vicissitudes of a life spent accumulating books, can probably guess without checking that in any given month, the Books Bought and Books Read lists hardly overlap.

Hornby's dispatches provide a surprising, stimulating, and inevitably hilarious tour through the contours of a deeply generous and good-natured intelligence. Hornby reads widely, with an inimitably affectionate and sardonic curiosity. The essays in this book guide readers toward great books in every genre, from fusty to pop, introducing works they may have overlooked, dismissed, or simply bought and forgot beneath a pile of other books.

Adding *More Baths Less Talking* to one's own Books Read list may renew one's energy for attacking a nearby pile of unconquered paperbacks, and should inspire a more forgiving attitude toward allowing those piles of unread books to grow a little higher. ✶

MORE
BATHS
LESS
TALKING

MAY 2010

It's never easy, returning home after failing to make one's way out in the world. When I left these pages in 2008, it was very much in the spirit of "Goodbye, nerdy losers! I'm not wasting any more time ploughing through books on your behalf! I have things to do, places to go, people to see!" Ah, well. What can you do, if the people don't want to be seen? I have now become that pathetic modern phenomenon you might have read about, the boomerang child—the kid who struts off (typically and unwisely with middle finger raised), spends a couple of years screwing up some lowly job on a magazine or in a bank, and then comes back, tail between his legs, to reclaim his old bedroom and wonder how come his parents have more fun than he on a Saturday night.

"What's a parent to do?" bewails a terrifying (for me) article dealing with this very issue on the website *eHow.com*. "It's hard to turn your children away. The best thing a parent can do is help them understand that they are adults now and the rules have changed." The new rules for parents, the piece goes on to say, should include charging rent and refusing to buy toiletries and other incidentals. I'm pretty sure I'm going to end up getting my own way on the incidental toiletries, should it come to that. It's pretty hot here at Believer Towers, and I suspect that the Polysyllabic Spree, the 115 dead-eyed but fragrant people who edit this magazine, will cave in long before I do. Still. It wasn't what I expected when I left: that eighteen months later, I'd be working for free deodorant. What's particularly humiliating in my case is that, unlike most boomerang children, I'm considerably older than those who have taken me back in. They're not as young as they were, the Spree, but even so.

I have decided to vent my spleen by embarking on a series of books that, I hope, will be of no interest whatsoever to the readership of this magazine. David Kynaston's superlative *Austerity Britain* is more than six hundred pages long and deals with just six years, 1945–51, in the life of my country. The second volume in the series, *Family Britain, 1951–57*, has already been published, so I plan to move on to that next; Kynaston is going to take us through to Margaret Thatcher's election in 1979, and I'm warning you now that I plan to read every single word, and write about them in great detail in this column.

I am less than a third of the way through *Austerity Britain*, but I have read enough to know that this is a major work of social history: readable, brilliantly researched, informative, and gripping. Part of Kynaston's triumph is his immense skill in marshaling the resources at his disposal: it seems at times as though he must have read every novel written in the period, and every autobiography, whether that autobiography was written by a member of the postwar Labour government or by a member of England's postwar cricket team. (On page 199 of my paperback, he quotes from former Labour deputy leader Roy Hattersley, Stones bassist Bill Wyman, and cookery writer Elizabeth David, all on the subject of the miserable, bitter winter of 1947.) And it goes without saying that he's listened to every radio program, and trawled through every newspaper.

The effect Kynaston achieves is extraordinary: Britain changes month by month, like a child, and you end up feeling that every citizen of the world should have the opportunity to read a book this good about their own country. I'm glad that not everyone in the U.K. has read it (although it has sold a lot of copies), because you can steal anecdotes from it and pass them off as your own. One of my favorites so far is David Lean's account of showing *Brief Encounter* at a cinema in Rochester, Kent, to a tough audience full of sailors from the nearby Chatham dockyards. "At the first love scene one woman down in the front started to laugh. I'll never forget it. And the second love scene it got worse. And then the audience caught on and waited for her to laugh and they all joined in and it ended in absolute shambles. They were rolling in the aisles." *Brief Encounter* is a much-loved British film, often taken out of a back pocket and waved about when someone wants to make a point about how we have changed as a nation, and what we have lost: in the old days, we spoke better, emoted less, stayed married, didn't get naked at the drop of a hat, etc. We are cursed with an apparently unshakable conviction that we are all much more knowing than people used to be, back in the Pre-Ironic Age, so it is both instructive and humbling to learn that, half a century ago, Rochester sailors didn't need the *Onion* to tell them what was hilarious.

The best stuff of all Kynaston has taken from Britain's extraordinary Mass Observation project, which ran from the late 1930s to the mid-'60s. The creators of MO—the anthropologist Tom

Harrisson, the poet Charles Madge, and the filmmaker Humphrey Jennings, among others (even the formidable, and formidably clever, literary critic William Empson was involved somewhere)—got five hundred volunteers to keep diaries or reply to questionnaires, and the results provide the best record of what the war and its aftermath meant to ordinary Britons. True, there were some peculiar types involved; Henry St. John, a civil servant living in Bristol, scrupulously described each opportunity for masturbation, as and when it arose. A visit to London's Windmill Theatre, famous for its nude tableaux vivants, elicits this observation: "I delayed masturbation until another para-nude appeared seen frontways, with drapery depending between the exposed breasts." The day after Hiroshima sees Henry returning to a public lavatory in the northeast "to see if I could masturbate over the mural inscriptions." Say what you like about the internet, but for a certain class of underemployed male, life has become warmer, and more hygienic.

It's not all about wanking, of course. *Austerity Britain* is about the morale of a battered, broke nation, and its attempts to restore itself; it's about food rationing and town planning, housing and culture, socialism and aspiration, and it never forgets for a second that its (mostly gray and brown) tiles make up a big, big mosaic of our tiny, beleaguered island. And if you read or write fiction, you may be gratified to see how Kynaston relies on the contemporary stuff to add color and authenticity to his portrait of the times. The received wisdom is that novels too much of the moment won't last; but what else do we have that delves so deeply into what we were thinking and feeling at any given period? In fifty or one hundred years' time, we are, I suspect, unlikely to want to know what someone writing in 2010 had to say about the American Civil War. I don't want to put you off, if you're just writing the last paragraph of a seven-hundred-page epic novel about Gettysburg—I'm sure you'll win loads of prizes and so on. But after that, you've had it.

It's been a month of enjoyment in unlikely places, if David Kynaston will forgive me for wondering whether an enormous nonfiction book with the word *austerity* in the title was going to be any fun. Francis Spufford's forthcoming novel, *Red Plenty*, is about Nikita Khrushchev's planned economy, and it contains the phrase (admittedly in the extensive footnotes at the back) "the multipliers on which Kantorovich's solution to optimisation problems depended," and it's terrific. Yes, reading it involves a certain amount of self-congratulation—"Look at me! I'm reading a book about shortages in the early '60s Soviet rubber industry, and I'm loving it!" But actually, such sentiments are entirely misplaced, and completely unfair to Spufford, who has succeeded in turning possibly the least-promising fictional material of all time into an incredibly smart, surprisingly involving, and deeply eccentric book, a hammer-and-sickle version of Altman's *Nashville*, with central committees replacing country music. (*Red Plenty* would probably make a marvelous film, but I'll let someone else pitch the idea to the Hollywood studio that would have to pay for it.) Spufford provides a terrific cast, a mixture of the real and the fictional, and hundreds of vignettes that illustrate how Khrushchev's honorable drive to bring enough of whatever was needed to his hungry and oppressed countrymen, impacted on the lives of economists, farmers, politicians, black-marketeers, and even hack writers. (There was, of course, no other type, seeing as you wrote what you were told to write.)

Francis Spufford's name has come up in this column before: his *The Child That Books Built* is a brilliant memoir about what we read when we're young and why. And though I am not alone in thinking that he has one of the most original minds in contemporary literature, there really aren't as many of us as there should be. His own fantastic perversity is to blame for this—apart from *Red Plenty* and the memoir, he's written books about ice and English boffins—but you always end up convinced that the fusty-looking subject he's picked is resonant in all sorts of ways that you couldn't possibly have foreseen. One of his themes here is the sheer brain-power required for the extraordinary experiment that was Soviet communism; we know now that it was an experiment that failed, but controlling all aspects of supply and demand is a lot more complicated than sitting back and letting the market sort every-thing out. It turns out that genius is required. Not quite as much was necessary for the conception, research, and writing of this extraordinary novel, but that's only because novels don't need as much as entire economic systems. Oh, come on. They really don't.

A year or so back, my coeditor and I selected a story by Philipp Meyer for a collection we were putting together. (It came out, this collection. It was one of the many moneymaking schemes of the last eighteen months that failed to make money. Short stories by mostly young, mostly unknown American writers! For publication in the U.K. only! What could have gone wrong? Nothing, that's what. Which is why I suspect that I've been diddled, and that my coeditor is currently snorting cocaine and buying racehorses in Florida.) It was pretty good, this story, so when I saw Meyer's first novel, *American Rust,* reviewed ecstatically in the *Economist,* of all places, I... well, I was going to say, self-aggrandizingly, that I hunted it down, like some kind of implacable bibliomaniac Mountie, but we all know that nowadays hunting books down takes about two seconds.

The cover of my copy of *American Rust* sports blurbs by both Patricia Cornwell and Colm Tóibín, which positions it very neatly: *American Rust* is one of those rare books that provides the reader with not only a big subject—the long, slow death of working-class America—but a gripping plot that tunnels us right into the middle of it. Isaac and Poe, early twenties, both have plans to escape their broken Pennsylvania town, full of rotting steel mills (the book is cry-ing out for a quote from Springsteen to go alongside those from Tóibín and Cornwell). Isaac is smart, and wants to go to a California college; Poe has been offered a sports scholarship that he's too unfo-cused to accept. And then Isaac kills someone, and it all goes to hell.

There is nothing missing from this book that I noticed, nothing that Meyer can't do. His characters are beautifully drawn and memorable—not just Isaac and Poe, but the sisters and parents and police chiefs, even the minor characters, the Dickensian drifters and petty criminals that Isaac meets during his flight from Pennsylvania. The plot is constructed in such a way that it produces all kinds of delicate moral complications, and none of this is at the expense of the book's sorrowful, truly empathetic soul. And, unlike most first novelists, Meyer knows that we're all going to die, and that before we do so we are going to mess our lives up somehow. There. I hope that's sold it to you.

You have to admit that when three books this good get read back to back, I'm the one that has to be given most of the credit. Yes, I appreciate the craft that has gone into these books, the research, the love, the patience, the imagination, the immense skill—just as I appreciate the craft that goes into the making of a perfectly spherical and lovingly stitched football. But, with the greatest of respect to Kynaston, Spufford, and Meyer, it's the reader who sticks the ball in the back of the net, the person who really counts. He shoots, he scores. Three times. A hat trick, in his first column back! He's still got it. ✶

JUNE 2010

So this last month, I went to the Oscars. I went to the Oscars as a <u>*nominee*</u>, I should stress (apparently in underlined italics), not as some loser, even though that, ironically, was what I became during the ceremony, by virtue of the archaic and almost certainly corrupt academy voting process. And my task now is to find a way of making the inclusion of that piece of information look relevant to a column about my reading life, rather than gratuitous and self-congratulatory. And I think I can do it, too: it strikes me that just about every book I've read in the past few weeks could be categorized as anti-Oscar. *Austerity Britain?* That one's pretty obvious. Both words in that title are antithetical to everything that happens in Hollywood during awards season. You're unlikely to catch a CAA agent in the lobby of the Chateau Marmont reading Andrew Brown's thoughtful, occasionally pained book about his complicated relationship with Sweden; Elif Batuman's funny, original *The Possessed: Adventures with Russian Books and the People Who Read Them* is populated by people who spend their entire lives thinking about, say, the short stories of Isaac Babel, rather than Jennifer Aniston's career. (I'm not saying that one mental occupation is superior to the other, but they're certainly different, possibly even oppositional.) And even Patti Smith's memoir, which could have been glamorous and starry, is as much about Genet and Blake as it is about rock and roll, and is suffused with a sense of purpose and an authenticity absent even from independent cinema. Oh, and no fiction at all, which has got to be significant in some way, no? If you want to ward off corruption, then surely the best way to do it is to sit by a swimming pool and read a chapter about Britain's postwar housing crisis. It worked for me, anyway. I can exclusively reveal that if you sit by a swimming pool in L.A., wearing swimming shorts and reading David Kynaston, then Hollywood starlets leave you alone.

Finishing *Austerity Britain* was indisputably my major achievement of the month, more satisfying, even, than sitting in a plush seat and applauding for three and a half hours while other people collected statuettes. A month ago I had read less than a third of the book, yet it was already becoming apparent that Kynaston's research, the eccentric depth and breadth of it, was going to provide more pleasure than one had any right to expect; there were occasions during the last few hundred pages when it made me laugh. At one point, Kynaston quotes a 1948 press release from the chairman of Hoover, and adds in a helpful parenthetical that it was "probably written for him by a young Muriel Spark." The joy that extra information brings is undeniable, but, once you get to know Kynaston, you will come to recognize the pain and frustration hidden in that word *probably:* how many hours of his life, you wonder, were spent trying to remove it?

While I was reading about the birth of our National Health Service, President Obama was winning his battle to extend health care in America; it's salutary, then, to listen to the recollections of the doctors who treated working-class Britons in those early days. "I certainly found when the Health Service started on the 5th July '48 that for the first six months I had as many as twenty or thirty ladies come to me who had the most unbelievable gynaecological conditions—I mean, of that twenty or thirty there would be at least ten who had complete prolapse of their womb, and they had to hold it up with a towel as if they had a large nappy on." Some 8 million pairs of free spectacles were provided in the first year, as well as countless false teeth. It's not that people were dying without free health care; it's that their quality of life was extraordinarily, needlessly low. Before the NHS, we were fumbling around half-blind, unable to chew, and swaddled in giant homemade sanitary napkins; is it possible that in twenty-first-century America, the poor are doing the same? Two of the most distinctive looks in rock and roll were provided by the NHS, by the way. John Lennon's specs of choice were the 422 Panto Round Oval; meanwhile, Elvis Costello favored the 524 Contour. What, you think David Kynaston would have failed to provide the serial numbers? Panto Round Oval, by the way, would be a pretty cool name for a band. Be my guest, but thank me in the acknowledgments.

My parents were in their twenties during the period covered in *Austerity Britain,* and it's easy to see why they and their generation went crazy when we asked for the simplest things—new hi-fis, chopper bikes, Yes triple-albums—when we were in our teens. They weren't lying; they really didn't have stuff like that when they were young. Some 35 percent of urban households didn't have a fixed bath; nearly 20 percent didn't have exclusive access to a toilet. One of the many people whose diaries provide Kynaston with the backbone to this book describes her father traveling from Leicester to west London, a distance of over a hundred miles, to watch the 1949 FA Cup Final, the equivalent of the Super Bowl back then. He didn't go all that way because he had a ticket for the game; it was just that he'd been invited to watch a friend's nine-inch black and white television. We stayed in the Beverly Wilshire for the Oscars, thank you for asking. It was OK.

I haven't read *Puzzled People*, the Mass Observation book published in 1947 about contemporary attitudes to spirituality, all the way through. (As I explained last month—please keep up—Mass Observation was a sociological experiment in which several hundred people were asked to keep diaries, and, occasionally, to answer questionnaires; the results have provided historians, including David Kynaston, with a unique source of information.) And you don't need to read the whole thing, anyway. The oblique first-person responses to metaphysical matters are ideal, if you have a spare moment to dabble in some found poetry—and who doesn't, really?—much as the surreality of the Clinton/Lewinsky testimony led to the brilliant little book *Poetry Under Oath* a few years back. ("I don't know / That I said that / I don't / I don't remember / What I said / And I don't remember / To whom I said it.") Here are a couple I made at home:

THE PURPOSE OF LIFE

Now you've caught me.
I've no idea.

My life's all work
And having babies.

Well, I think we're all cogs
Of one big machine.

What I'm wondering is,
What is the machine for?

That's your query.

JESUS

I wouldn't mind
Being like Him

But he was too good.

Didn't he say
"Be ye perfect"
Or something like that?

Well,
That's just
Ridiculous

I bought *Fishing in Utopia* because I found myself in a small and clearly struggling independent village-bookshop, and I was desperate to give the proprietor some money, but it was a struggle to find anything that I could imagine myself reading, among all the cookbooks and local histories. And sometimes imagination is enough. Surely we all occasionally buy books because of a daydream we're having—a little fantasy about the people we might turn into one day, when our lives are different, quieter, more introspective, and when all the urgent reading, whatever that might be, has been done. We never arrive at that point, needless to say, but *Fishing in Utopia*—quirky, obviously smart, quiet, and contemplative—is exactly the sort of thing I was going to pick up when I became someone else. By reading it now, I have got ahead of myself; I suspect that the vulgarity of awards season propelled me into my own future.

And in any case, the Sweden that Andrew Brown knew in the late '70s and early '80s is not a million miles, or even forty years, away from Austerity Britain. Our postwar Labour government was in some ways as paternalistic, and as dogged and dour in its pursuit of a more egalitarian society, as Olof Palme's Social Democrats, and one can't help but feel a sense of loss: there was a time when we were encouraged to think and act collectively, in ways that were not always designed to further individual self-interest. In England after the war, no TV was shown between the hours of six and eight p.m., a hiatus that became known as the Toddler's Truce; the BBC decided that bedtime was stressful enough for parents as it was, and, as there was only one TV channel in the U.K. until 1955, childless viewers were left to twiddle their thumbs. In Olof Palme's Sweden, you bought booze in much the same way as you bought pornography: furtively, and from the back of a shady-looking shop. It would be nice to think that we have arrived at our current modus vivendi—children watching thirty-plus hours of TV a week, young people with a savage binge-drinking problem, in the U.K. at least—after prolonged national debates about individual liberty versus the greater good, but of course it just happened, mostly because the free market wanted it to. I may not have sold *Fishing in Utopia* to you unless you are at least a bit Swedish and/or you like casting flies. But Andrew Brown demonstrates that any subject under the sun, however unpromising, can be riveting, complex, and resonant, if approached with intelligence and an elegant prose style. He even throws in a dreamy, mystical passage about the meaning and consolations of death, and you don't come across many of those.

Despite my affection for my German publishers, and for Cologne, the city in which my German publishers live, I wasn't particularly looking forward to reading at LitCologne, the hugely successful literary festival that takes place there every March. I had been traveling a lot (I was actually nominated for an Academy Award this year, believe it or not, and that necessitated quite a lot of schlepping around), and the novel I was reading from feels as though it came out a lifetime ago, and I hadn't written anything for the best part of a year. And then, the morning after my reading, I was in Cologne Cathedral with Patti Smith and our German editor, admiring the beautiful new Gerhard Richter window, and I remembered what's so great about literary festivals: stuff like that usually happens. It's not always Patti Smith, of course, but it's frequently someone interesting, someone whose work has meant a lot to me over the years, and I end up wondering what I could possibly have written in these twenty-four hours that would have justified missing out on the experience. I started *Just Kids* on the plane home and finished it a couple of days later.

Like Dylan's *Chronicles*, it's a riveting analysis of how an artist ended up the way she did (and as I get older, books about the sources of creativity are becoming especially interesting to me, for reasons I don't wish to think about), and all the things she read and listened to and looked at that helped her along the way. And it was a long journey, too. Smith arrived in New York in the summer of '67, and her first album was released in 1975. In between there was drawing, and then poetry, and then poetry readings with a guitar, and then readings with a guitar and a piano... And yet this story, the story of how a New Jersey teenager turned into Patti Smith, is only a subplot, because *Just Kids* is about her relationship with Robert Mapplethorpe, the young man she met on her very first day in New York City, fell in love with, lived with, and remained devoted to for the rest of his short life. One of the most impressive things about *Just Kids* is its discipline: that's Smith's subject, and she sticks to it, and everything else we learn about her comes to us through the prism of that narrative.

There is a lot in this book about being young in New York in the 1970s—the Chelsea Hotel, Warhol and Edie Sedgwick, Wayne

County and Max's Kansas City, Tom Verlaine and Richard Lloyd, Gregory Corso and Sam Shepard. And of course one feels a pang, the sort of ache that comes from being the wrong age in the wrong place at the wrong time. The truth is, though, that many of us—most of us—could have been right outside the front door of Max's Kansas City and never taken the trouble (or plucked up the courage) to open it. You had to be Patti Smith, or somebody just as committed to a certain idea of life and how to live it, to do that. I felt a different kind of longing while reading *Just Kids*. I wanted to go back to a time when cities were cheap and full of junk, and on every side street there was a shop with dusty windows that sold radiograms and soul albums with the corners cut off, or secondhand books that nobody had taken the trouble to value. (Smith always seems to be finding copies of *Love and Mr Lewisham* signed by H. G. Wells, or complete sets of Henry James, the sale of which pays the rent for a couple of weeks.) Now it's just lattes and bottles of banana foot lotion, and it's difficult to see how banana foot lotion will end up producing the Patti Smiths of the twenty-first century; she needed the possibilities of the city, its apparently inexhaustible pleasures and surprises. Anyway, I loved *Just Kids*, and I will treasure my signed hardback until I die—when, like all my other precious signed first editions, it will be sold by my sons, for much less than it will be worth, probably to fund their gambling habits. And then, perhaps, it will be bought secondhand by a rocking boho in some postcapitalist thrift store on Fifth Avenue or Oxford Street, and the whole thing will start up all over again. ✶

JULY/AUGUST 2010

If you are reading this in the U.S., the presumption over here in the U.K. is that you have either just come out of a session with your shrink or you're just about to go into one, and for reasons best known to ourselves, we disapprove—in the same way that we disapprove of the way you sign up for twelve-step programs at the drop of a hat, just because you're getting through a bottle of vodka every evening after work and throwing up in the street on the way home. "That's just life," we say. "Deal with it." (To which you'd probably reply, "We are dealing with it! That's why we've signed up for a twelve-step program!" So we'd go, "Well, deal with it in a less self-absorbed way." By which we mean, "Don't deal with it at all! Grin and bear it!" But then, what do we know? We're smashed out of our skulls most of the time.)

Recently I read an interview with a British comic actress, an interesting, clever one, and she articulated, quite neatly, the bizarre assumptions and prejudices of my entire nation when it comes to the subject of the talking cure. "I have serious problems with it... The way I see it is that you're paying someone, so they don't really care about you—they're not listening in the way that someone who loves you does."

There's a good deal in that little lot to unpack. The assumption that if you give someone money, then, ipso facto, they don't care about you, is a curious one; the chief complaint I have about my dentist is that he cares too much, and as a consequence is always telling me not to eat this or smoke that. According to the actress, he should just be laughing all the way to the bank. And how does she feel about child care? Maybe she can't bring herself to use it, but in our house we're effectively paying someone to love our kids. (Lord knows, it wouldn't happen any other way.) But the real zinger is in that second argument, the one about "not listening in the way that someone who loves you does." Aaaargh! Der! D'oh! That's the whole point, and to complain that therapists aren't friends is rather like complaining that osteopaths aren't pets.

One of the relationships described in *Who Is It That Can Tell Me Who I Am?*, psychotherapist Jane Haynes's gripping, moving, and candid memoir, is clearly a defining relationship in her life, a love affair in all but the conventional sense. The affair is between Haynes and her own therapist, and the first half of the book is addressed to him; he died before their sessions had reached a conclusion, and Haynes's grief is agonizing and raw. So much for the theory that a bought relationship can't be real. In the second half of the book, Haynes describes the problems and the breakthroughs of a handful of her patients, people paralyzed by the legacies of their personal histories, and only the most unimaginative and Gradgrindian of readers could doubt the value of the therapeutic process. Pills won't work for the patient whose long, sad personal narrative has produced an addiction to internet pornography; pills didn't work for the woman who was saved from suicide, tragicomically, only because of a supermarket bag she placed over her head after she'd taken an overdose. (The maid cleaning her hotel room would have presumed she was sleeping had it not been for the fact that her face was obscured by an advertisement for Tesco.) As Hilary Mantel says in her quite-brilliant introduction, we don't enter the consulting room alone, "but with our parents and grandparents, and behind them, jostling their ghost limbs for space, our ancestral host, our tribe. All these people need a place in the room, all need to be heard. And against them, our own voice has to assert itself, small and clear, so that we possess the narrative of our own lives." In a bravura passage, Mantel goes on to describe what those narratives might read like: "For some of us, they are a jerky cinema flickering against a rumpled bedsheet, the reels out of order and the projectionist drunk. For some of us they are slick and fake as an old dance routine, all high kicks and false smiles and a desperate sweat inside an ill-fitting costume... For others, the narrative is the patter of a used-car salesman, a promise of progress and conveyance, insistently delivered with an oily smirk... There is a story we need to tell, we think: but this is not how; this is not it." If you think you can find a friend who is prepared to listen hour after hour, year after year, to your painful, groping attempt to construct your own narrative, then good luck to you. Me, I have friends who are prepared to listen for ten minutes to my list of which players Arsenal Football Club needs to mount a serious challenge next year—but then, I'm an English bloke. My therapist, however, has tolerated more agonized, baffled nonsense than any human being should endure. And yes, I pay him, but not enough.

Perhaps unsurprisingly, given the tenor of Mantel's introduction and the nature of psychotherapy itself, with its painfully slow storyboarding of life's plot twists, there is a good deal in this book about the value of literature. Haynes repeatedly claims that she'd find her job impossible without it, in fact—that Shakespeare and Tolstoy, J. M. Barrie (there's an extraordinary passage from *Peter Pan* quoted here, hence its appearance in Books Bought), and Chekhov have all created grooves that our narratives frequently wobble into, helpfully, illuminatingly. So even if you have no time for Jung and Freud, there's something for the curious and literate *Believer* reader, and as I can't imagine there's any other kind, then this book is for you. It's occasionally a little self-dramatizing, but it's serious and seriously smart, and Haynes allows her patients a voice, too: Callum, the young man addicted to pornography, makes an incidental but extremely important observation about the "pandemic" that the internet has helped spread among men of his generation. (Haynes quotes the psychoanalyst Joan Raphael-Leff, who says that sex "is not merely a meeting of bodily parts or their insertion into the other but *of flesh doing the bidding of fantasy*." So what does it say about those who use pornography, I wonder, that they are prepared to spend so much time watching the insertion of body parts?) I'm going to stop banging on about this book now, but I got a lot out of it. As you can probably tell.

In 1971, the Booker Prize suddenly changed its qualification period. Up until then, the prize had been awarded to a work of fiction published in the previous twelve months; in '71 they switched it, and the award went to a book released contemporaneously. In other words, novels published in 1970 weren't eligible for the prize. So somebody has had the bright idea of creating a Lost Booker Prize for this one year, and as a consequence our bookstores are displaying a short list of novels that, if not exactly forgotten (they had to be in print to qualify), certainly weren't terribly near the top of British book-club reading lists—and I'm betting not many of you have read Nina Bawden's *The Birds on the Trees*, J. G. Farrell's *Troubles*, *The Bay of Noon* by Shirley Hazzard, *Fire from Heaven* by Mary Renault, *The Driver's Seat* by Muriel

Spark, or Patrick White's *The Vivisector.* I bought three of them, partly because it was such a pleasure to see books published forty years ago on a table at the front of a chain store: British bookshops are desperately, crushingly dull at the moment. Our independents are almost all gone, leaving bookselling at the mercy of the chains and the supermarkets, and they tend to favor memoirs written, or at least approved, by reality-TV stars with surgically enhanced breasts, and recipe books by TV chefs. To be honest, even memoirs written in person by reality-TV stars with entirely natural breasts wouldn't lift the cultural spirits much. If asked to represent this magazine's views, I'd say we favor natural breasts over augmented, but that breasts generally are discounted when we come to consider literary merit. And if I have that wrong, then I can only apologize.

Nina Bawden's *The Birds on the Trees* is what became known, a few years later, as a Hampstead Novel—Hampstead being a wealthy borough of London that, in the imagination of some of our grumpier provincial critics, is full of people who work in the media and commit adultery. My wife grew up there, and she works in the media, but… Actually, I should do some fact-checking before I finish that sentence. I'll get back to you. Nobody would dare write a Hampstead novel anymore, I suspect, and though its disappearance is not necessarily a cause for noisy lamentation—there is only so much to say about novelists having affairs, after all—it's interesting to read an early example of the genre. *The Birds on the Trees* is about a middle-class media family (the wife is a novelist, the husband a journalist) in the process of falling apart, mostly because of the stress brought on by a son with mental-health problems. People drink a lot of spirits. Marshall McLuhan is mentioned, and he doesn't come up so much in fiction anymore. There are lots of characters in this short book, all with tangled, knotty connections to each other—it feels like a novel-shaped Manhattan at times—and, refreshingly, Bawden doesn't feel the need to be definitive. There's none of that sense of "If you read one book this year, make it this one"; you get the sense that it was written in an age where people consumed new fiction as a matter of course, so there was no need to say everything you had to say in one enormous, authoritative volume.

None of the Lost Booker books are very long; I chose to read Muriel Spark's *The Driver's Seat* (a) because I'd never read anything by Muriel Spark before, and she has the kind of reputation that convinced me I was missing out and (b) her novel was so slim that it is almost invisible to the naked eye. And, if you look at the Books Bought and Books Read columns this month, you will see, dear youthful writer, that short books make sound economic and artistic sense. If Spark had written a doorstopper of a novel, I probably wouldn't have bought it; if I'd bought it, I wouldn't have gotten around to picking it up; if I'd picked it up, I wouldn't have finished it; if I'd finished it, I'd have chalked her off my to-do list, and my relationship with Muriel Spark would be over. As it is, she's all I read at the moment, and the income of her estate (she died four years ago) is swelling by the day. What's the flaw in this business plan? There isn't one.

My only caveat is that your short novels have to be really, really good—that's the motor for the whole thing. (If you're going to write bad short books, then forget it—you'd be better off writing one bad long one.) *The Driver's Seat,* which is pitched straight into the long grass somewhere between Patricia Highsmith and early Pinter, is a creepy and unsettling novella about a woman who travels from Britain to an unnamed European city, apparently because she is hell-bent on getting herself murdered. I couldn't really tell you why Spark felt compelled to write it, but understanding the creative instinct isn't a prerequisite for admiring a work of art, and its icy strangeness is part of its charm. *A Far Cry from Kensington* came later but is set earlier, in a West London boardinghouse whose inhabitants are drawn toward each other in strange ways when one of them, an editor at a publishing house, is rude to a talentless hack. (She calls him a *"pisseur de copie,"* an insult that is repeated gleefully and satisfyingly throughout the book. Spark is fond of strange, funny mantras.) *The Prime of Miss Jean Brodie* is her most famous novel, at least here, where the movie, starring Maggie Smith as an overbearing and eccentric teacher in a refined Scottish girls' school, is one of our national cinematic treasures. I probably enjoyed this last one the least of the three—partly because I'd seen the film, partly because Miss Brodie is such a brilliantly realized archetype that I felt I'd already come across several less-successful versions of her. (Influential books are often a disappointment, if they're properly influential, because influence cannot guarantee the quality of the imitators, and your appetite for the original has been partially sated by its poor copies.) But what a writer Spark is—dry, odd, funny, aphoristic, wise, technically brilliant. I can't remember the last time I read a book by a well-established writer previously unknown to me that resulted in me devouring an entire oeuvre—but that only brings me back to the subject of short books, their beauty and charm and efficacy. *A Far Cry from Kensington* weighs in at a whopping 208 pages, but the rest are all around the 150 mark. You want your oeuvre devoured? Look and learn.

At the end of *The Prime of Miss Jean Brodie,* one of Miss Brodie's girls, now all grown up, visits another, and attempts to tell her about her troubled marriage. "'I'm not much good at that sort of problem,' said Sandy. But Monica had not thought she would be able to help much, for she knew Sandy of old, and persons known of old can never be much help." Which sort of brings us full circle.

In next month's exciting episode, I will describe an attempt, not yet begun, to read *Our Mutual Friend* on a very modern ebook machine thing. It's the future. Monday, in fact, probably, once more Spark oeuvre has been devoured. ★

SEPTEMBER 2010

BOOKS BOUGHT:

* Our Mutual Friend—
  Charles Dickens
* Brooklyn: Historically
  Speaking—
  John B. Manbeck

BOOKS DOWNLOADED
FOR NOTHING:

* Our Mutual Friend—
  Charles Dickens
* The Adventures of
  Huckleberry Finn—
  Mark Twain
* Babbitt—Sinclair Lewis

BOOKS READ:

* Live From New York:
  An Uncensored History of
  Saturday Night Live
  —Tom Shales and James
  Andrew Miller
* Brooklyn—Colm Tóibín
* The Girls of Slender
  Means—Muriel Spark
* The Given Day—
  Dennis Lehane (half)
* Loitering With Intent—
  Muriel Spark (half)
* The Finishing School—
  Muriel Spark (half)
* Tinkers—Paul Harding
  (one-third)

Four years ago to the very month, as I'm sure you will remember, this column daringly introduced a Scientist of the Month award. The first winner was Matthias Wittlinger, of the University of Ulm, in Germany, who had done remarkable things with, and to, ants. In an attempt to discover how it was that they were able to find their way home, Wittlinger had shortened the legs of one group and put another group on stilts, in order to alter their stride patterns. Shortening the legs of ants struck us, back in 2006, as an entirely admirable way to spend one's time—but we were younger then, and it was a more innocent age. Despite the huge buzz surrounding the inaugural award,

Wittlinger received nothing at all, and is unlikely even to know about his triumph, unless he subscribes to this magazine. And to add insult to injury, there was no subsequent winner, because the following month we forgot about the whole thing.

Anyway: it's back! I am absurdly pleased to announce that this month's recipient, Rolando Rodríguez-Muñoz, is employed at a university right here in England, the University of Exeter. Together with his colleague Tom Tregenza, Rodríguez-Muñoz has been studying the mating strategies of crickets; they discovered, according to the *Economist,* that "small males... could overcome the handicap of their stature and win mates through prodigious chirping." In other words, being the lead singer works for the nerdy and the disadvantaged in other species, too.

Rodríguez-Muñoz has shaded it over Tregenza because, after he and his colleagues had "captured, marked, released and tracked hundreds of crickets," they filmed sixty-four different cricket burrows; Rodríguez-Muñoz watched and analyzed the results, two hundred and fifty thousand hours of footage. A quarter of a million hours! Just under three years of cricket porn! Presumably crickets, like the rest of us, spend much more time trying to get sex than actually having it, but even so, he must have seen some pretty racy stuff. Some of the sterner members of the judging panel tried to argue that because Rolando had watched the film on fast-forward, and on sixteen monitors at once, he had cut corners, but I'm not having that; as far as I'm concerned, watching crickets mate quickly is even harder than watching them mate in normal time. No, Rolando Rodríguez-Muñoz is a hero, and fully deserving of all the good things about to come his way.

There was a hurtful suggestion, four years ago, that the Scientist of the Month was somehow tangentially connected to the World Cup. He hasn't read enough to fill up a whole column, because he's spent the entire month watching TV, the argument went; so just because he stumbled upon an interesting article in a magazine between games, he's invented this bullshit to get him out of a hole. I resent this deeply, not least because it devalues the brilliant work of these amazing scientists. And though it is true that, at the time of writing, we are approaching the end of another World Cup, and reading time has indeed been in shorter supply, I can assure you that the sudden reappearance of this prestigious honor is pure, though admittedly baffling, coincidence.

The effect of the World Cup on the books I intended to read has been even more damaging in 2010 than it was in 2006. In '06, I simply didn't pick any up, and though I was troubled by the ease with which a game between Turkey and Croatia could suppress my hunger for literature, at least literature itself emerged from the tournament unscathed. This time around, as you can see from the list above, my appetite was partially satisfied by grazing on the first few pages of several books, and as a consequence, there are half-chewed novels lying all over the place. At least, I'm presuming they're lying all over the place; I seem to have temporarily lost most of them. When the World Cup is over, and we clear away the piles of betting slips and wall charts, some of them will, presumably, reappear. I wrote in this column recently about Muriel Spark's novels, their genius and their attractive brevity, but there is an obvious disadvantage to her concision: her books tend to get buried under things. I can put my hands on Dennis Lehane's historical novel *The Given Day* whenever I want, simply because it is seven hundred pages long. True, this hasn't helped it to get itself read, but at least it's visible. I didn't lose *The Girls of Slender Means,* and it was as eccentric and funny and sad as the bunch of Spark novels I read last month.

At the end of the last column, I vowed to have read *Our Mutual Friend* on an e-reader, and that didn't happen either. This was partly because of the football, and partly because the experience of reading Dickens in this way was unsatisfactory. It wasn't just that a Victorian novelist clearly doesn't belong on a sleek twenty-first-century machine; I also took the cheapskate route and downloaded the novel from a website that allows you to download out-of-copyright novels for no charge. I helped myself to *Babbitt* and *The Adventures of Huckleberry Finn* at the same time. The edition squirted down to me came without footnotes, however, and I rather like footnotes. More to the point, I *need* footnotes occasionally. (You may well work out for yourself eventually that the "dust" so vital to the plot is household rubbish, rather than fine grains of dirt, but it saves a lot of confusion and doubt to have this explained clearly and plainly right at the beginning of the novel.) The advantage handed the e-reading business by copyright laws hadn't really occurred to me before I helped myself, but it spells trouble for publishers, of course; Penguin and Co. make a lot of money selling books by people who are long dead, and if we all take the free-downloading route, then there will be less money for the living writers. In a spirit of self-chastisement, I bought a copy of *Our Mutual Friend* immediately, even though I have one somewhere already. It won't do any good, in the long run, because clearly books, publishers, readers, and writers are all doomed. But maybe we should all do what we can to stave off impending disaster just that little bit longer.

I was attempting to read *Our Mutual Friend* for professional reasons: I'm supposed to be writing an introduction for a forthcoming edition. I read Colm Tóibín's *Brooklyn* for work, too: I was asked to consider taking on the job of adapting it for the cinema, and as about a million critics and several real people had told me how good it was, I took the offer seriously. It's not the best circumstance in which to read a novel. Instead of admiring the writing, thinking about the characters, turning the page to discover what happens next, you're thinking, Oh, I dunno, and, Yay, I could chop that, and, Miley Cyrus would be *great* for this, and, Do I really want to spend the next few years of my life wrecking this guy's prose? It is a tribute to Tóibín's novel—its quiet, careful prose, its almost agonizing empathy for its characters, its conviction in its own reality—that pretty soon I forgot why I was reading it, and just read it. And then, after I'd finished it, I decided that I wanted to adapt it—not just because I loved it, but because I could see it. Not the movie, necessarily, but the world of the novel: the third-class cabin in which his protagonist travels from Liverpool to New York in the early 1950s, the department store she works in, the dances she attends. They are portrayed with a director of photography's relish for depth and light and detail.

The laziest, most irritating book-club criticism of a novel is that the reader "just didn't care" about the characters or their predicament, a complaint usually made in a tone suggesting that this banality is the product of deep and original thought. (It never seems to occur to these critics that the deficiency may well lie within themselves, rather than in the pages of the books. Perhaps they feel similarly about their friends, parents, children. "The trouble with my kid is that she doesn't make me *care* enough about her." Are we all supposed to nod sagely at that?)

It is not intended to be a backhanded compliment when I say that Tóibín doesn't care whether you care about Eilis, his heroine; it's not that the book is chilly or neutral, or that Tóibín is a disengaged writer. He's not. But he's patient, and nerveless, and unsentimental, and he trusts the story rather than the prose to deliver the emotional payoff. And it does deliver. *Brooklyn* chooses the narrative form of a much cheaper kind of book—"one woman, two countries, two men"—but that isn't what it's about; you're not quite sure what it's about until the last few pages, and then you can see how carefully the trap has been laid for you. I loved it. Will I wreck it? It's perfectly possible, of course. It's a very delicate piece, and Eilis is a watchful, still center. I won't have to hack away at its complicated architecture, though, because it doesn't have one, so maybe I have half a chance. By the time you read this, I should have started in on it; if you have a ten-year-old daughter with ambitions to be an actor, then she might as well start trying to acquire an Irish accent. In my experience of the film business, we'll be shooting sometime in 2020, if it hasn't all collapsed by then.

In a way, I read *Live From New York,* an oral history of *Saturday Night Live,* because of work, too. Earlier in the year I got an American agent, a lovely, smart woman whose every idea, suggestion, and request I've ignored, more or less since the moment we agreed she'd represent me. Anyway, she recommended Tom Shales and James Andrew Miller's book, and my feeling was that if I'm not going to make her a penny, I could at least follow up on her book tips. And I'm pretty sure that if it had to be one or the other, money or successful recommendations, she'd go for the recommendations. That's what makes her special.

I read the book despite never having seen a single minute of *Saturday Night Live,* at least prior to Tina Fey's turn as Sarah Palin in 2008. The show was never shown in the U.K., so I hadn't a clue who any of these people were. Will Ferrell? Bill Murray? Adam Sandler? Eddie Murphy? John Belushi? Chris Rock? Dan Aykroyd? It's sweet that you have your own TV stars over there. You've probably never heard of Pat Phoenix, either.

When it's done well, as it is here, then the oral history is pretty unbeatable as a nonfiction form—engrossing, light on its feet, the constant switching of voices a guarantee against dullness. Legs McNeil's *Please Kill Me: The Uncensored Oral History of Punk,* George Plimpton's Edie Sedgwick book, Studs Terkel's *Working*... These are books that I hope to return to one day, when I've read everything else. *Live From New York* is probably just a little too long for someone unfamiliar with the show, but if you want to learn something about the crafts of writing and performing, then you'll pick something up every few pages. I am still thinking about these words from Lorne Michaels:

> The amount of things that have to come together for something to be good is just staggering. And the fact that there's anything good at

all is just amazing. When you're young, you assume that just knowing the difference between good and bad is enough: "I'll just do good work, because I prefer it to bad work."

Michaels's observation contains a terrible truth: you think, at a certain point in your life, that your impeccable taste will save you. As life goes on, you realize it's a bit more complicated than that.

While I was reading *Live From New York,* I realized that G. E. Smith, the show's musical director, was the same G. E. Smith who sat next to me on a plane from New York to London, sometime in 1976 or 1977. I was just returning to college after visiting my dad; Smith was on tour with Daryl Hall and John Oates, who were up in first class. He was the first musician I'd ever met, and he was charming, and generous with his time. And he sold me on *Abandoned Luncheonette,* Hall and Oates's heartstoppingly lovely folk–soul album, recorded well before the disco years (which were pretty good, too, actually). He wouldn't remember a single second of them, but the conversations we had on that flight helped feed the idea, just sprouting then, that I didn't want a proper job. It was a pretty seminal flight, now that I come to think about it. I still love *Abandoned Luncheonette.* ✶

OCTOBER 2010

BOOKS BOUGHT:
* *Hellhound on His Trail:*
  The Stalking of Martin
  Luther King, Jr. and the
  International Hunt for His
  Assassin—
  Hampton Sides
* *The Broken Word*—
  Adam Foulds
* *It Happened in Brooklyn:*
  An Oral History of
  Growing Up in the
  Borough in the 1940s,
  1950s, and 1960s—
  Myrna Katz Frommer
  and Harvey Frommer

* *How to Live: Or, a Life*
  of Montaigne in One
  Question and Twenty
  Attempts at an Answer—
  Sarah Bakewell
* *Barney's Version*—
  Mordecai Richler

BOOKS READ:
* *Hard Rain Falling*—Don
  Carpenter
* *The Conversations: Walter*
  Murch and the Art of
  Editing Film—Michael
  Ondaatje
* *Tinkers*—Paul Harding

O n the day I arrived at last year's Sundance Film Festival, amid the snow and the painfully cold sponsored parties, I met a screenwriter who wanted to talk, not about movies or agents or distribution deals, but about this column, and this column only. Given the happy relationship between books and film, and the mutual understanding between authors and those who work in the movie industry, I presumed that this would be the first of many such conversations about the *Believer;* indeed, I was afraid that, after a couple of days, I would begin to tire of the subject. I didn't want to be asked, over and over again, what the members of the Polysyllabic Spree were really like, in real life; I wanted the chance to offer my opinion on Miramax's troubles, or the potential weaknesses in the new setup at WME. I made it my policy from that moment on to engage only with people who didn't look like *Believer* readers. It was a policy that proved to be amazingly successful.

So Michael was the one who slipped under the wire, and I'm glad he did. He wanted one shot at a book recommendation—presumably on the basis of the fact that my own had ruined his reading life over the last few years—and hit me with John Williams's novel *Stoner*. (To my relief, the title turned out to refer to a surname rather than an occupation.) *Stoner* is a brilliant, beautiful, inexorably sad, wise, and elegant novel, one of the best I read during my grotesquely unfair suspension from these pages. So when Michael, emboldened by his triumph, came back with a second tip, I listened, and I bought.

Don Carpenter's *Hard Rain Falling* is, like *Stoner,* part of the NYRB Classics series, but it didn't begin its life, back in 1966, wearing that sort of smart hat. Search the title in Google Images and you'll find a couple of the original covers, neither of which give the impression that Carpenter could read, let alone write. One shows a very bad drawing of a hunky bad boy leaning against the door of his jail cell; the other is a little murky on my screen, but I'm pretty sure I can see supine nudity. And of course these illustrations misrepresent Carpenter's talents and intentions, but they don't entirely misrepresent his novel: if you'd paid good money for it back in '66, in the hope that (in the immortal words of Mervyn Griffith-Jones, the hapless chief prosecutor at the Lady Chatterley trial in 1960) you might be picking up something that you wouldn't want your wife and servants to read, then you wouldn't have asked for your money back.

A lot of books containing descriptions of sex have been written since the 1960s, and I pride myself on having read at least part of every single one of them, but there was something about Carpenter's novel that dated the dirty bits, and sent me right back to my 1960s childhood. Every now and again, I would, if I delved deep enough in the right drawers, come across books that my father had hidden carefully away—John Cleland's *Fanny Hill,* for example, first published in 1749, but still being read surreptitiously, in the U.K. at least, over two hundred years later. (Wikipedia tells me that *Fanny Hill* was banned in the U.K. until 1970, but I found the family edition long before that, so I don't know where my father got his copy. He has gone up even further in my estimation.) We are long past the time when literature was capable of doubling as pornography, and I doubt whether twenty-first-century teenage boys with access to a computer bother riffling through *The Godfather* and Harold Robbins paperbacks as assiduously as I did in the early '70s. These days, regrettably, sex in novels must contain a justifying subtext; what dates the coupling in Carpenter's novel is that, some of the time at least, the couples concerned are simply enjoying themselves. I can't remember the last time I read a description in a literary novel of a couple doing it just for fun. (And if you have written exactly such a novel yourself, I am happy for you, and congratulations, but please don't send it to me. It's too late now.)

Hard Rain Falling is a hard-boiled juvenile-delinquent novel, and then a prison novel, and then a dark Yatesian novel of existential marital despair, and just about every metamorphosis is compelling, rich, dark but not airless. Carpenter is, at his best, a dramatist: whenever there is conflict, minor characters, dialogue, people in a poolhall or a cell or a bed, his novel comes thrillingly alive. The energy levels, both mine and the book's, dipped a little when Carpenter's protagonist Jack Levitt finds himself in solitary confinement, where he is prone to long bouts of sometimes-crazed introspection. Form and content are matched perfectly in these passages, but that doesn't make them any more fun to read. Most of the time, though, *Hard Rain Falling* is terrific—and if you're reading this, Michael, then I'd like you to know you have earned a third recommendation.

I finished *Hard Rain Falling* in Dorset, in a wonderful disused hotel which pitches its atmosphere halfway between *Fawlty Towers* and *The Shining*'s Overlook. I was there with family and friends, and, though I never forgot that I am a reader—I read, which helped to remind me—I completely forgot that I am a writer. This meant that the flavor of *The Conversations,* a collection of Michael Ondaatje's erudite, stimulating, surprising interviews with the film editor Walter Murch, was different from what it would have been had I devoured it during the rest of the year. In these pages a couple of months ago, I said that books about creativity and its sources are becoming increasingly important to me as I get older, but this has to be something connected with work—when I read these books (Patti Smith's memoir was the most recent, I think) I try to twist them into a shape that makes some kind of sense to me professionally. There is so much that is of value to writers in *The Conversations;* any book about film editing that manages to find room for the first and last drafts of Elizabeth Bishop's "One Art," in their entirety, has an ambition and a scope that elude most books about poetry. If I'd been in a different mode—in the middle of a novel, say—I'd have been much more alert to the book's value as a professional aid; and just occasionally, something that one of these two clever men said would jerk me out of my vacation and back to my computer all those miles away. Murch's reference to "Negative Twenty Questions," for example, a game invented by the quantum physicist John Wheeler to explain how the world looks at a quantum level and much too complicated to tell you about here... something about the way Murch used the game to illustrate the process of film editing dimly reminded me of how writing a book feels, if you end up plotting on the hoof.

But mostly I read the book simply as someone who has seen a lot of films, and as Murch edited *Apocalypse Now* and *The Godfather* and *The Conversation* and *The English Patient* (and reedited Welles's *Touch of Evil* using the fifty-eight-page memo that Welles wrote to the studio after he'd seen the studio's cut of the film), then I was in experienced hands: this book is a dream, not just for cineasts, but for anyone interested in the tiny but crucial creative decisions that go into the making of anything at all. At one point, Murch talks about recording the sound of a door closing in *The Godfather*—a film, you suddenly remember, whose entire meaning rests on the sound of a door closing, when Michael excludes Diane Keaton from the world he promised he'd never join. If Murch had gotten that wrong, and the door had closed with a weedy, phony click, then it's entirely possible that we wouldn't still be reading about his career today. And there's tons of stuff like that, discussions that seem like the nerdy fetishization of trivia, until the import of that trivia becomes clear. Harry Caul in *The Conversation* was going to be called Harry Caller (after *Steppenwolf*'s Harry Haller), until he decided that "Caller" was an insufficiently oblique name for a professional bugger. So "Caller" became "Call," which became "Caul" after a secretary's misprint, which in turn gave Coppola the idea of dressing Gene Hackman in his distinctive semitransparent raincoat. And Murch is reminded of this by a story of Ondaatje's about W. H. Auden, who saw that a misprint in a proof produced a line better than his original: "The poets know the name of the seas" became "The ports know the name of the seas"… Oh, boy. If you're who I think you are, you would love *The Conversations*. Strangely, though, every friend I've pressed it upon so far has already read it, which suggests (a) that it's clearly one of those books whose reputation has grown and grown since it was first published, in 2002, and (b) my friends think I'm some kind of dimbo who only reads football reports and the lyrics of Black Sabbath songs.

And, in any case, it turns out that editing is kind of a metaphor for living. Our marriages, our careers, our domestic arrangements… so much of how we live consists of making meaning out of a bewildering jumble of images, of attempting to move as seamlessly as we can from one stage of life to the next.

There comes a time in the life of every young writer of fiction when he or she thinks, I'm not going to bother with plot and character and meaningless little slivers of human existence—I've done all that. I'm going to write about *life itself*. And the results are always indigestible, sluggish, and pretentious. If you're lucky, you get this stage over with before you're published—you have given yourself permission to rant on without the checks of narrative; if you're unlucky, it's your publisher who has given you enough rope with which to hang yourself, usually because your previous book was a brilliant success, and it can be the end of you.

Tinkers is Paul Harding's first novel, and it's pretty much about life itself, and it won him the Pulitzer Prize; he got away with it because he has a poet's eye and ear, and, because he's a ruthless self-editor, and because he hasn't forgotten about his characters' toenails and kidneys even as he's writing about their immortal souls. (That's just an overexcited figure of speech, by the way, that bit about toenails and kidneys. There are no toenails in *Tinkers,* that I remember. I don't want to put anyone off.) Harding was at the Iowa Writers' Workshop, and I don't know whether he was taught by Marilynne Robinson, but if he was, then I would have loved to sit in on their tutorials; *Tinkers,* in its depth, wisdom, sadness, and lightly worn mysticism, is reminiscent of Robinson's *Housekeeping.* (And I'm not suggesting for a moment he ripped her off, because you can't rip Marilynne Robinson off, unless you too are wise and deep and possessed of a singular and inimitable consciousness.)

Tinkers is about a dying man called George Crosby; he's an old man, coming to the end of his natural life, and he's hallucinating and remembering, failing to prevent the past from leaking into the present. And George's dying is linked to his father, Howard's, life, and eventual death. Howard sold household goods off the back of a wagon toward the beginning of the last century—he was a tinker. George repaired clocks. It's breathtakingly ambitious in its simplicity, but Harding is somehow able, in this novel that runs less than two hundred pages, to include the moments on which a life turns, properly imagined moments, moments grounded in the convincing reality of the characters. I was going to say that it's perhaps not the best book to take on holiday, because who wants to be reminded of his own mortality while he watches his children frolicking in the icy British surf? But then again, who wants to be reminded of his own mortality after he's wasted a day messing around on the internet instead of writing a very small section of a superfluous novel, or a screenplay that probably won't get turned into a film? On reflection, the holiday option is probably the better one: when my time comes, I hope that my children frolic before my eyes. I certainly don't want to see an unedited paragraph of a superfluous novel. ✷

NOVEMBER/DECEMBER 2010

Something has been happening to me recently—something which, I suspect, is likely to affect a significant and important part of the rest of my life. The grandiose way of describing this shift is to say that I have been slowly making my peace with antiquity; or, to express it in words that more accurately describe what's going on, I have discovered that some old shit isn't so bad.

Hitherto, my cultural blind spots have included the Romantic poets, every single bar of classical music ever written, and just about anything produced before the nineteenth century, with the exception of Shakespeare and a couple of the bloodier, and hence more Tarantinoesque, revenge tragedies. When I was young, I didn't want to listen to or read anything that reminded me of the brown and deeply depressing furniture in my grandmother's house. She didn't have many books, but those she did own were indeed brown: cheap and old editions of a couple of Sir Walter Scott's novels, for example, and maybe a couple of hand-me-down books by somebody like Frances Hodgson Burnett. When I ran out of stuff to read during the holidays, I was pointed in the direction of her one bookcase, but I wanted bright Puffin paperbacks, not mildewed old hardbacks, which came to represent just about everything I wasn't interested in.

This unhelpful association, it seems to me, should have withered with time; instead, it has been allowed to flourish, unchecked. Don't you make yogurt by putting a spoonful of yogurt into something-or-other? Well, I created a half century of belligerent prejudice with one spoonful of formative ennui. I soon found that I didn't want to read or listen to anything that anybody in any position of educational authority told me to. Chaucer was full of woodworm; Wordsworth was yellow and curling at the edges, whatever edition I was given. I read Graham Greene and John Fowles, Vonnegut and Tom Wolfe, Chandler and Nathanael West, Greil Marcus and Peter Guralnick, and I listened exclusively to popular music. Dickens crept in, eventually, because he was funny, unlike Sir Walter Scott and Shelley, who weren't. And, because everything was seen through the prism of rock and roll, every now and again I would end up finding something I learned about through the pages of *New Musical Express.* When Mick Jagger happened to mention that "Sympathy for the Devil" was inspired by Bulgakov's *The Master and Margarita,* off I trotted to the library. It didn't help that I was never allowed to study anything remotely contemporary until the last year of university: there was never any sense of *that* leading to *this.* If anything, my education gave me the opposite impression, of an end to cultural history round about the time that Forster wrote *A Passage to India.* The quickest way to kill all love for the classics, I can see now, is to tell young people that nothing else matters, because then all they can do is look at them in a museum of literature, through glass cases. Don't touch! And don't think for a moment that they want to live in the same world as you! And so a lot of adult life—if your hunger and curiosity haven't been squelched by your education—is learning to join up the dots that you didn't even know were there.

In some ways, my commitment to modernity stood me in good stead: those who cling to the cultural touchstones of an orthodox education are frequently smug, lazy, and intellectually timid—after all, someone else has made all their cultural decisions for them. And in any case, if you decide to consume only art made in the twentieth century and the first part of the twenty-first, you're going to end up familiar with a lot of good stuff, enough to last you a lifetime. If your commitment to the canon means you've never had the time for Marilynne Robinson or Preston Sturges or Marvin Gaye, then I would argue that you're not as cultured as you think. (Well, not you. You know who Marvin Gaye is. But they're out there. They're out here, in Britain, especially.)

Over the last couple of years, though, I've been dipping into Keats's letters, listening obsessively to Saint-Saëns, seeking out paintings by van Eyck, doing all sorts of things that I'd never have dreamed of doing even in my forties; what is even more remarkable, to me, at least, is that none of these things feel alien. There wasn't one single Damascene moment. Rather, there was a little cluster of smaller discoveries and awakenings, including:

1. Laura Cumming's magnificent book *A Face to the World: On Self-Portraits,* one of the cleverest, wisest books of criticism I've ever read. I wouldn't have picked it up in a million years if I hadn't known the author, and I ended up chasing after the self-portraits she writes about, which involved visiting galleries and old masters I'd carefully avoided until she taught me not to. (I read this book during my laughably unjust and almost certainly illegal suspension from these pages

last year, so I was unable to recommend it to you then, but you should read it.)

2. The Professor Green/Lily Allen song "Just Be Good to Green." I am old enough to remember not only the Beats International version, "Dub Be Good to Me," but the SOS Band's original, "Just Be Good to Me." And I'm not saying that the Professor sent me off screaming toward Beethoven's late quartets (very good, by the way); I did, however, find myself wondering whether, when a song keeps coming round again and again and again, like a kid on a merry-go-round, there comes a point when you have to stop smiling and waving. Saint-Saëns is a new artist, as far as I'm concerned, with a big future ahead of him.

3. A new pair of headphones, expensive ones, which seemed to me to be demanding real food, orchestras and symphonies, rather than a wispy diet of singer-songwriter.

4. Jane Campion's beautiful film *Bright Star,* which turned Keats into a writer I recognized and understood.

5. During promotional work for *Lonely Avenue,* the project I've been working on with Ben Folds, the two of us were asked to trade tracks for some iTunes thing. Ben recommended an early Elton John album and the first movement of Rachmaninoff's Third Piano Concerto. I bought the Rachmaninoff, because the enthusiasm was so unaffected and unintimidating.

6. And now, Sarah Bakewell's biography of Montaigne, *How to Live.*

I had never read Montaigne before picking up Bakewell's book. I knew only that he was a sixteenth-century essayist, and that he had therefore willfully chosen not to interest me. So I am at a loss to explain quite why I felt the need first to buy and then to devour *How to Live*. And it was a need, too. I have talked before in these pages about how sometimes your mind knows what it needs, just as your body knows when it's time for some iron, or some protein, or a drink that doesn't contain caffeine or absinthe. I suspect in this case the title helped immeasurably. This book is going to tell me how to live, while at the same time filling in all kinds of gaps in my knowledge? Sold.

Well, *How to Live* is a superb book, original, engaging, thorough, ambitious, and wise. It's not just that it provides a handy guide to Hellenic philosophy, and an extremely readable account of the sixteenth-century French civil wars; you would, perhaps, expect some of that, given Montaigne's influences and his political involvement. (He became mayor of Bordeaux, a city that had been punished for its insurrectionist tendencies.) Nor is it that it contains immediate and sympathetic portraits of several of Montaigne's relationships—with his wife, his editor, and his closest friend, La Boétie, who died in one of the frequent outbreaks of the plague, and of whom Montaigne said, famously, "If you press me to tell why I loved him, I feel that this cannot be expressed, except by answering: Because it was he, because it was I." The conventional virtues of a biography are all there, and in place, but where Bakewell really transcends the genre is in her organization of the material, and her refusal to keep Montaigne penned in his own time. In just over three hundred pages, she provides a proper biography, one that takes into account the hundreds of years he has lived since his death; that, after all, is when a lot of the important stuff happens. And the postmortem life of Montaigne has been a rich one: he troubled Descartes and Pascal, got himself banned in France (until 1854), captivated and then disappointed the Romantics, inspired Nietzsche and Stefan Zweig, made this column possible.

He did this by inventing the medium of the personal essay, more or less single-handedly. How many other people can you think of who created an entire literary form? Indeed, how many people can you think of who created any cultural idiom? James Brown, maybe; before "Papa's Got a Brand New Bag" there was no funk; and then, suddenly, there it was. Well, Montaigne was the James Brown of the 1580s. In his brilliant book *A Year in the Life of William Shakespeare: 1599,* James Shapiro says that Montaigne took "the unprecedented step of making himself his subject," thus enabling Shakespeare to produce a dramatic equivalent, the soliloquy. Of course, you can overstate the case for Montaigne's innovative genius. It's hard to imagine that, in the five-hundred-odd years since the essays were first published, some other narcissist wouldn't have had the idea of sticking himself into the middle of his prose. Montaigne invented the personal essay like someone invented the wheel. Why he's still read now is not because he was the first, but because he remains fresh, and his agonized agnosticism, his endearing fumbles in the dark (he frequently ends a thought or an opinion with a disarming, charming "But I don't know"), become more relevant as we realize, with increasing certainty, that we don't have a clue about anything. I'd be surprised and delighted if I read a richer book in the next twelve months.

And then, as if Montaigne's hand were on my shoulder, I discovered Emily Fox Gordon's *Book of Days,* a collection of personal essays. I had read a nice review of them in the *Economist,* but had presumed that they'd be nicely written, light, amusing, and disposable, but that's not it at all: these are not blogs wrapped up in a nice blue cover. (And is it OK, given the *Believer's* no-snark rule, to say that some blogs are better than others? And that one or even two have no literary merit whatsoever?) There are jokes in *Book of Days,* but the writing is precise, the thinking is complicated and original, and just about every subject she chooses—faculty wives, her relationship with Kafka, her niece's wedding—somehow enables her to pitch for something rich and important. If you are interested in writing and marriage—and if you're not, then I don't know what you're doing round here, because I got nothing else, apart from kids and football—then she has things to say that I have never read elsewhere, and that I will be thinking about and possibly even re-reading for some time to come. In Sarah Bakewell's introduction to *How to Live,* she quotes the English journalist Bernard Levin: "I defy any reader of Montaigne not to put the book down at some point and say with incredulity, 'How did he know all that about me?'" Well, I haven't yet had that experience with Montaigne, probably because in my admittedly limited excursions so far, I've been looking for the smutty bits, but I felt it several times while I was reading *Book of Days.* "The Prodigal Returns," the essay about Gordon's niece's wedding, turns into a brilliant meditation on the ethics and betrayals of memoir-writing, and contains the following:

> What *do* I enjoy? Not staying in hotels, apparently. Not gluttony, not parties, not flattery, not multiple glasses of white wine. What I seem to want to do—"enjoy" is the wrong word here—is not to have experiences but to think and tell about them. I'm always looking for excuses to avoid sitting down at my desk to write, but I "enjoy" my life only to the extent that even as I'm living it, I'm also writing it in my mind.

Well. Obviously that's not me, in any way whatsoever. I'm an adventurer, a gourmand, a womanizer, a *bon viveur,* a surfer, a bungee jumper, a gambler, an occasional pugilist, a Scrabble player, a man who wrings every last drop from life's dripping sponge. But, you know. I thought it might chime with one or two of you lot. Nerds. And it certainly would have chimed with Montaigne.

I'm afraid I am going to recommend yet another epic poem about the Mau Mau uprising—this time Adam Foulds's extraordinary and pitch-perfect *The Broken Word*. It will occupy maybe an hour of your life, and you won't regret a single second of it. Foulds has written an apparently brilliant novel, *The Quickening Maze,* about the poet John Clare, in whom I have obviously had no previous interest, but this has the narrative drive of a novel anyway. Set in the 1950s (*der,* say the people who know all about the Mau Mau, which I'm presuming isn't every single one of you), it tells the story of Tom, a young Englishman who, in the summer between school and university, goes to visit his parents in Kenya, and is drawn into a horrific, nightmarish suppression of a violent rebellion. If there were money to be made from cinematic adaptations of bloody, politically aware but deeply humanistic long-form poetry, then the film rights to *The Broken Word* would make Foulds rich.

Such is his talent that Foulds can elevate just about any banal domestic conversation. In the last section of the poem, Tom is attempting to seduce a young woman at university, and the dialogue is full of *nos* and *that's not nices,* the flat, commonplace rejections of a 1950s courtship. But what gives the passage its chilling power is everything that has gone before: how much of the violence Tom has seen is contained in him now? The control here is such that the language doesn't have to be anything other than humdrum to be powerful, layered, dense, and that's some trick to pull off. Why the Mau Mau uprising? At the end of the poem, Tom and the girl he has been forcing himself upon are looking in a jeweler's window; the children they would have had together, born at the end of the 1950s and early '60s, sent to English public schools, are as we speak running our banks and our armies, our country, even.

These are three of the best books I've read in years, and I read them in the last four weeks, and they are all contemporary—*How to Live* and *Book of Days* were published in 2010, *The Broken Word* was published in 2008. So despite all my showing off and name-dropping, a narrative poem published two years ago and set in the 1950s is the closest I've come to the ancient world. But then, that's the whole point, isn't it? Great writing is going on all around us, always has done, always will. ✷

JANUARY 2011

BOOKS BOUGHT:
* ⋆ *Dickens Dictionary*— Alexander J. Philip
* ⋆ *Half a Life*— Darin Strauss
* ⋆ *The Anthologist*— Nicholson Baker
* ⋆ *The Million Dollar Mermaid*— Esther Williams

BOOKS READ:
* ⋆ *Our Mutual Friend*— Charles Dickens
* ⋆ *The Uncoupling*— Meg Wolitzer
* ⋆ *Let the Great World Spin*—Colum McCann
* ⋆ *Half a Life*— Darin Strauss

The advantages and benefits of writing a monthly column about reading for the *Believer* are innumerable, if predictable: fame, women (it's amazing what people will do to get early information about the Books Bought list), international influence, and so on. But perhaps the biggest perk of all, one that has only emerged slowly, over the years, is this: you can't read long books. Well, I can't, anyway. I probably read between two and three hundred pages, I'm guessing, during the average working week, and I have the impression—please correct me if I'm wrong—that if you saw only one book in the Books Read list at the top there, it would be very hard to persuade you to plough through what would, in effect, be a two-thousand-word book review. And as a consequence, there are all sorts of intimidating-looking eight-hundred-pagers that I feel completely justified in overlooking. I am ignoring them for your benefit, effectively, although it would be disingenuous to claim that I spend my month resenting you. On the contrary, there have been times when, watching friends or fellow passengers struggling through some au courant literary monster, I have wanted to kiss you. I once gave a whole column over to *David Copperfield,* I remember, and more recently I raced through David Kynaston's brilliant but Rubenesque *Austerity Britain.* For the most part, though, there's a "Stuff I've Been Reading"–induced five-hundred-page cutoff.

In the interests of full disclosure, I should add that I am a literary fattist anyway; I have had a resistance to the more amply proportioned book all my adult life, which is why the thesis I'm most likely to write is entitled "The Shortest Book by Authors Who Usually Go Long." *The Crying of Lot 49, Silas Marner, A Portrait of the Artist as a Young Man*... I've read 'em all. You can infer from that lot what I haven't read. And in any case, long, slow books can have a disastrous, demoralizing effect on your cultural life if you have young children and your reading time is short. You make only tiny inroads into the chunky white wastes every night before falling asleep, and before long you become convinced that it's not really worth reading again until your children are in reform school. My advice, as someone who has been an exhausted parent for seventeen years now, is to stick to the svelte novel—it's not as if this will lower the quality of your consumption, because you've still got a good couple of hundred top, top writers to choose from. Have you read everything by Graham Greene? Or Kurt Vonnegut? Anne Tyler, George Orwell, E. M. Forster, Carol Shields, Jane Austen, Muriel Spark, H. G. Wells, Ian McEwan? I can't think of a book much over four hundred pages by any of them. I wouldn't say that you have to make an exception for Dickens, because we at the *Believer* don't think that you have to read anybody—we just think you have to read. It's just that short Dickens is atypical Dickens—*Hard Times,* for example, is long on angry satire, short on jokes—and Dickens, as John Carey said in his brilliant little critical study *The Violent Effigy: A Study of Dickens' Imagination,* is "essentially a comic writer." If you're going to read him at all, then choose a funny one. *Great Expectations* is under six hundred pages, and one of the greatest novels ever written, so that's not a bad place to start.

Some months ago, I agreed to write an introduction to *Our Mutual Friend*—eight or nine hundred pages in paperback form, a terrifying two-and-a-half thousand pages on the iPad—and I have been waiting for a gap in the *Believer's* monthly schedule before attempting to embark on the long, long road. The recent double issue gave me an eight-week window of opportunity to read Dickens's last completed novel (only the unfinished *The Mystery of Edwin Drood* came after it) on top of something else, so I knew I couldn't put it off any longer.

I first read *Our Mutual Friend* years and years ago, and didn't enjoy the experience much, but I was almost certain that the fault was mine rather than the author's. Something was going on at the time—divorce, illness, a newborn, or one of the other humdrum hazards that turn reading into a chore—and *Our Mutual Friend* never really started to move in the way that the other big Dickens novels had previously done. (There's this moment you get a hundred or so pages in, if you're lucky and sympathetic to Dickens's narrative style and worldview, when you feel the whole thing judder into life and pick up speed, like a train, or a liner, or some other vehicle whose size and weight make motion seem unlikely.) So I didn't worry about taking on the commission. I am in reasonable health, my next divorce is at least a year or so away, and I have given up having children, so I was sure that, this time around, I'd see that *Our Mutual Friend* is right up there with the other good ones—in other words, I was about to read one of the richest, most inventive, funniest, saddest, most energetic novels in literature.

Two-thirds of the way through, I was having such a hard time that I looked up a couple of contemporary reviews. Henry James thought it "the poorest of Mr Dickens's works... poor with the poverty not of momentary embarrassment, but of permanent exhaustion." Dickens's loyal friend John Forster admits that it "will never rank with his higher efforts." In other words, everyone knew it was a clunker except me—and even I knew, deep down, given that my first reading had been so arduous. And now, presumably, I have to write an introduction explaining why it's so great. What's great is the fifth chapter, an extended piece of comic writing that's as good as anything I've ever read by him. (If you have a copy lying about, start it and end it there, as if it were a Wodehouse short story.) What's not so great about it is not so easy to convey, because so much of it relates—yes—to length, to the plot's knotty overcomplications, stretched over hundreds and hundreds of pages. "Although I have not been wanting in industry, I have been wanting in invention," Dickens wrote to Forster sadly, after the first couple of parts had already been published in magazine form, and, as a summation of what's wrong with the book as a whole, that confession is hard to beat. It's interesting, I think, that nothing in *Our Mutual Friend* has wandered out of the pages of the novel and into our lives. There's no Artful Dodger, Uriah Heep, or Micawber, no Scrooge, no Gradgrind, no "It was the best of times, it was the worst of times," no Miss Havisham, no *Jarndyce v. Jarndyce*. The closest we get is a minor character saying, apropos of another character's gift for storytelling, that "he do the Police in different voices"—but Dickens needed a little help from Eliot for that particular stab at immortality. As far as I can tell, the novel has recovered from its poor reception, to the extent that it has become one of Dickens's most studied books, but that, I'm afraid, is no testament to its worth: it has endless themes and images and things to say about greed and poverty and money—in other words, endless material for essays—but none of that makes it any easier to get through. He'll be back in my life soon enough, but next time I might go for early Dickens, rather than late.

It now seems a very long time ago that I read Meg Wolitzer's forthcoming novel, *The Uncoupling,* and Colum McCann's National Book Award winner, *Let the Great World Spin,* and trying to think about them now is like trying to look over a very high wall into somebody's back garden. I know I enjoyed them, and they both seemed to slip by in a flash, but Dickens stomped his oversize boots all over them. I'm hoping that eventually they will spring back up in my mind, undamaged, like grass. McCann's novel, as many of you probably know, is set in New York City in August 1974, the summer that Philippe Petit walked between the Twin Towers on a tightrope. Underneath him, and all touched in some way by Petit's act of inspired insanity, lives McCann's cast of priests and lawyers, prostitutes and grieving mothers. It's a rich, warm, deeply felt and imagined book, destined, I think, to be loved for a long time. Regrettably, however, McCann makes a very small mistake relating to popular music toward the beginning, and, as has happened so many times before, I spent way too long muttering at both the novel and the author. I must stress, once again—because this has come up before—that my inability to forgive negligible errors of this kind is a disfiguring disease, and I am determined to find a cure for it; I mention it here merely to explain why a book I liked a lot has not become a book that I have bought over and over again, to press on anybody who happens to be passing by. And it would be unforgivably small-minded to go into it... Ach. Donovan wasn't an Irish folk singer, OK? He was a Scottish hippie, and I hate myself.

Meg Wolitzer, like Tom Perrotta, is an author who makes you wonder why more people don't write perceptive, entertaining, unassuming novels about how and why ordinary people choose to make decisions about their lives. Take away the historical fiction, and the genre fiction, and the postmodern fiction, and the self-important attention-seeking fiction, and there really isn't an awful lot left;

the recent success, on both sides of the Atlantic, of David Nicholls's lovely *One Day* demonstrates what an appetite there is for that rare combination of intelligence and recognizability. *The Uncoupling* is about what happens when all the couples in a New Jersey town stop having sex. (A magical wind, which springs up, not coincidentally, during rehearsals for a high-school production of Aristophanes's sex-strike comedy, *Lysistrata,* freezes the loins of all the post-pubescent women.) It's a novel that can't help but make you think about your own relationship—about what it consists of, what would be left if sex were taken away, how far you'd be prepared to go in order to keep it in your life somewhere, and so on. I have written all the answers to these questions down on a piece of paper, but I have locked the paper away in a drawer, and I'm not showing it to you lot. You know how much I get paid for this column? Not enough, that's how much.

The only thing I have read since Mr. and Mrs. John Harmon moved into Boffin the Golden Dustman's splendid house—that's an *Our Mutual Friend* spoiler, by the way, but I'm hoping I've spoiled it for you already—is Darin Strauss's *Half a Life,* a book that, as far as I'm concerned, could easily be republished under the title *The Opposite of Our Mutual Friend.* It's a short, simple piece of contemporary nonfiction, which in itself would be enough to make it look pretty good to me; it also happens to be precise, elegantly written, fresh, wise, and very sad. Strauss was still in high school when he killed a girl in an accident: Celine Zilke, then aged sixteen, and a student at the same high school, inexplicably veered across two lanes before riding her bike right across his Oldsmobile. She died later, in the hospital. Strauss was completely exonerated by everybody concerned, but, for obvious human reasons, the accident came to define him, and *Half a Life* is a riveting attempt to articulate the definition.

Any moral or ethical objection you might have to *Half a Life*—what right has he got to produce a book out of this when that poor girl was the victim?—is dealt with very quickly, because, in part, *Half a Life* deals with the question of what right Strauss had to do anything at all. Was it OK to go back to school, laugh, go to the movies, look at anyone, feel sorry for himself, go to Celine's funeral, avoid her friends, talk to her parents, leave his bedroom? The author, a teenage boy, didn't have the answers to any of these questions, and they continued to elude him until well into adulthood. You could describe *Half a Life* as an elevated study of self-consciousness, in all senses of the compound noun—a book about a man watching his younger self watching his own every move, thought, feeling, checking and rechecking them before allowing them to escape into a place where they can be watched by other people—at which point the checking and rechecking start all over again. It's easy enough for us to say that what happened to Darin Strauss was a tragedy—not, of course, as big a tragedy as the one that befell Celine Zilke and her family, but a tragedy nonetheless. Easy enough for us to say, impossible for him to say—and therein lies Strauss's rich and meaningful material, material he works into a memorable essay. "Whatever you do in your life, you have to do it twice as well now," Celine Zilke's mother told him at the funeral. "Because you are living it for two people." Most of us can't live our lives well enough for one, but the care and thought that have gone into every line of *Half a Life* are indicative not only of a very talented writer, but of a proper human being.

And now Strauss has got me at it. I was going to end with a very good, if overcomplicated, joke about Dickens and a pair of broken Bose headphones, but I'm no longer sure it's appropriate. So I'll stop here. ✶

FEBRUARY 2011

It's a wet Sunday morning, and I'm sitting on a sofa reading a book. On one side of me is my eldest son, Danny, who is seventeen and autistic. His feet are in my lap, and he's watching a children's TV program on his iPad. Or rather, he's watching a part of a children's TV program, over and over again: a song from *Postman Pat* entitled "Handyman Song." Danny is wearing headphones, but I've just noticed that they're not connected properly, so I can hear every word of the song anyway. On my other side is another son, my eight-year-old, Lowell. He's watching the Sunday-morning football-highlights program *Goals on Sunday*. I'm caught between them, trying to finish Nicholson Baker's *The Anthologist*.

"Look at this, Dad," Lowell says.

He wants me to watch Johan Elmander's goal for Bolton at Wolves, the second in a 3–2 win. It's one of the best goals of the season so far, and at the time of writing has a real chance of winning the BBC's Goal of the Month award, but I only have thirteen pages of the novel to go, so I only glance up for a moment.

"Close the book," Lowell says.

"I saw the goal. I'm not going to close the book."

"Close the book. You didn't see the replay."

He tries to grab the book out of my hand, so we wrestle for a moment while I turn the corner of the page down. I watch the replay. He's satisfied. I return to *The Anthologist,* football commentary in one ear and the *Postman Pat* song in the other.

Would Nicholson Baker mind? I'm pretty sure he wouldn't choose for me to be reading his work under these circumstances, and I'm with him all the way. I'd rather be somewhere else, too. I'd rather be on a sun-lounger in southern California, in the middle of a necessarily childless reading tour, just for the thirty minutes it's going to take me to get to the end of the novel. I would savor every single minute of the rest of a wet English November Sunday with three sons, just so long as I was given half an hour—not even that!—of sunshine and solitude. I hope Baker would be pleased by my determination and absorption, though. I wasn't throwing his book away by submitting it to the twin assaults of *Postman Pat* and *Goals on Sunday.* I was hanging on to it for dear life.

It's a wonderful novel, I think, unusual, generous, educational, funny. The eponymous narrator, Paul Chowder, is a broke poet whose girlfriend has just left him; he's trying to write an introduction to an anthology of verse while simultaneously worrying about the rent and the history of rhyme. Chowder loves rhyme: he thinks that the blank verse of modernism was all a fascist plot, and that Swinburne was the greatest rhymer "in the history of human literature." Indeed, *The Anthologist* is full of artless, instructive digressions about all sorts of people (Swinburne, Vachel Lindsay, Louise Bogan) and all sorts of things (iambic pentameter) that I knew almost nothing about. Chowder might be an awful mess, but you trust him on all matters relating to poetry.

I developed something of a crush on Elizabeth Bishop after reading *The Anthologist*. I downloaded an MP3 of her reading "The Fish," and on an overnight work trip to Barcelona I took with me a copy of Bishop's collected poems but no clean socks, which is exactly the sort of thing that Paul Chowder might have done. I would say that in my half century on this planet so far, I have valued clean socks above poetry, so *The Anthologist* may literally have changed my life, and not in a good way. Luckily, it turns out that you can buy socks in Barcelona. Nice ones, too.

Pretty much everything I have read in the last month is related to the production of art and/or entertainment. Unlike all the others, Colm Tóibín's *Brooklyn* is not *about* art (and don't get sniffy about Céline Dion until I tell you what Carl Wilson has to say about her); it's about a young girl emigrating to the U.S. from a small town in Ireland in the 1950s. But as I am currently attempting to adapt *Brooklyn* for the cinema, it would be disingenuous to claim that the production of art and/or entertainment didn't cross my mind while I was re-reading it.

I haven't read a novel twice in six months for decades, and the experience was illuminating. It wasn't that I had misremembered anything, particularly, nor (I like to think) had I misunderstood much, first time around, but I had certainly forgotten the proximity of narrative events in relation to each other. Some things happened sooner than I was prepared for, and others much later—certainly much later than I can hope to get away with in a screenplay. You can do anything in a novel, provided the writing is good enough: you can introduce rounded, complex characters ten pages from the end, you can gloss over years in a paragraph. Film is a clumsier and more literal medium.

One thing that particularly struck me this time around is that though Tóibín's prose is precise and calm and controlled, *Brooklyn* is not an internal book. This is good news for a screenwriter, in most ways, but it did occur to me that if you strip away, as I have to do, all the control, then the story becomes alarmingly visceral. When Eilis travels third class on a ship to New York and ends up getting violently seasick and expelling her dinner through every available orifice... Well, if we show that on-screen, it will lose Tóibín's Jamesian poise. What you'll see, in fact, is a poor girl shitting copiously into a bucket. And Colm's devoted fans, aesthetes all, will say, Jesus, what has this hooligan done to our beautiful literary novel? There might be art riots, in fact, similar to those that greeted *The Rite of Spring* when it was first performed, in 1913. People will throw stuff at me, and I'll be running out of the premiere shouting, "*There was diarrhea in the book!*," but nobody will believe me. I'm going to blame the director. Who made the *Porky's* movies? We should hire him.

The invention of the iPad means, as I'm sure you have discovered by now, that you can watch Preston Sturges movies pretty well anywhere you want. I have seen *Sullivan's Travels, The Lady Eve,* and *The Palm Beach Story,* and though *Sullivan's Travels* remains my favorite, the minor characters in *The Palm Beach Story* are Dickensian in their weirdness and detail. It occurred to me that I know a lot more about, say, Montaigne and Richard Yates, having read very good books about them, than I do about Preston Sturges—a regrettable state of affairs, seeing as Sturges means more to me than either.

After reading Sarah Bakewell's brilliant *How to Live: A Life of Montaigne in One Question and Twenty Attempts at an Answer,* I came to understand how Montaigne invented soul-searching; after reading Blake Bailey's *A Tragic Honesty: The Life and Work of Richard Yates,* I saw why Yates's books are so incredibly miserable. Well, Donald Spoto's *Madcap: The Life of Preston Sturges* tells you everything you need to know about the pace of Sturges's movies: he lived that fast himself. He hung out with Isadora Duncan and Marcel Duchamp, took a job as assistant stage manager on Duncan's production of *Oedipus Rex,* traveled throughout Europe, ran branches of his mother's cosmetics company in New York and London, turned down a job as a one-hundred-dollar-a-week gigolo, and was honorably discharged from the U.S. military. And then he turned twenty-one, and things got really interesting.

Sturges didn't really start writing until he was thirty; he began work on his first successful play, *Strictly Dishonorable,* on June 14, 1929, and finished it on June 23. (According to his diary, he did no work on the fifteenth, sixteenth, or twenty-second.) He received a telegram from a producer on July 2 suggesting an August production, and *Strictly Dishonorable* was one of the biggest Broadway hits of the 1930s. It made him a fortune. Even so, we here at the *Believer* recommend a ten- or fifteen-year gestation period for a first novel, play, or screenplay, five years of writing, and then another five years of rewriting and editing. ("June 23: *Strictly Dishonorable* finished 5.40 this afternoon. Will polish tonight. Later: did so and drew set plans.") Yes, Sturges went on to write and direct *Sullivan's Travels,* and in 1947 was paid more than either William Randolph Hearst or Henry Ford II. But the slow, careful approach is unarguably more authentic and artistic, and will almost certainly result in a literary prize, or at least a nomination. (In defense of your creative-writing professors, Sturges did write a lot of stinkers for the stage. Robert Benchley, in the *New Yorker,* observed that "the more young Mr. Preston Sturges continues to write follow-ups to *Strictly Dishonorable,* the more we wonder who wrote *Strictly Dishonorable.*" You're not allowed to write cruel lines like that in this magazine, which is the only reason why I don't.)

I had no idea that Sturges's life had been so dizzyingly eventful; no idea, either, that he had changed the history of cinema by becoming the first Hollywood writer/director. He crashed and burned pretty spectacularly, too. He sank every dollar he had and a few hundred thousand more into a money-pit of a club; and after a hot streak of seven good-to-great films between 1940 and 1944, it was effectively all over for him by 1949. He made only one more, apparently very bad, movie before he died, in 1959. Spoto's book can't help but zip along, although I did find myself skipping over the synopses of some of Sturges's Broadway farces. Farce, it seems to me, is curiously resistant to synopsis: "He then makes his move to seduce Isabelle, but the judge enters, claiming it's his birthday and everyone must have champagne... The opera singer then reenters with pajamas for Isabelle... Gus puts pajama top over her head, and as it slips down her teddy falls to the floor..." I am sure that, in 1930, *Strictly Dishonorable* was the hottest ticket in town, and that had I been alive to see it, I'd have promptly died laughing. But nothing, I fear, can bring the magic back to life now.

It is not stretching a point to say that the rapidly shifting sands of critical and popular approbation are the subject of Carl Wilson's brilliant extended essay about Céline Dion, *Let's Talk About Love: A Journey to the End of Taste,* another in the excellent 33 ⅓ series. Most of the others I've read (with the exception of Joe Pernice's novella inspired by the Smiths' *Meat Is Murder*) are well-written but conventional songs of praise to an important album in rock's history—*Harvest, Dusty in Memphis, Paul's Boutique,* and so on. This one is different. Wilson asks the question: Why does everyone hate Céline Dion? Except, of course, it's not everyone, is it? She's sold more albums than just about anyone alive. Everyone loves Céline Dion, if you think about it. So actually, he asks the question: why do I and my friends and all rock critics and everyone likely to be reading this book and magazines like the *Believer* hate Céline Dion? And the answers he finds are profound, provocative, and leave you wondering who the hell you actually are—especially if, like many of us around these parts, you set great store by cultural consumption as an indicator of both character and, let's face it, intelligence. We are cool people! We read Jonathan Franzen and we listen to

Pavement, but we also love Mozart and *Seinfeld*! Hurrah for us! In a few short, devastating chapters, Wilson chops himself and all of us off at the knees. "It's always other people following crowds, whereas my own taste reflects my specialness," Wilson observes.

Let's Talk About Love belongs on your bookshelf next to John Carey's *What Good Are the Arts?;* they both cover similar ideas about the construct of taste, although Wilson finds more room for Elliott Smith and the Ramones than Professor Carey could. And in a way, taking on Dion is a purer and more revealing exercise than taking on some of the shibboleths of literary culture, as Carey did. After all, there is a rough-and-ready agreement on literary competence, on who can string a sentence together and who can't, that complicates any wholesale rejection of critical values in literature. In popular music, though, a whole different set of judgments is at play. We forgive people who can't sing or construct a song or play their instruments, as long as they are cool, or subversive, or deviant; we do not dismiss Dion because she's incompetent. Indeed, her competence may well be a problem, because it means she excludes nobody, apart from us, and those who invest heavily in cultural capital don't like art that can't exclude: it's confusing, and it doesn't help us to meet attractive people of the opposite sex who think the same way we do.

Wilson's book isn't just important; it has good facts in it, too. Did you know that in Jamaica, Céline is loved most of all by the badasses? "So much that it became a cue to me to walk, run or drive faster if I was ever in a neighborhood I didn't know and heard Céline Dion," a Jamaican music critic tells Wilson. And did you know that the whole highbrow/middlebrow thing came from nineteenth-century phrenology, and has racist connotations? Why aren't I surprised?

I may well have to insist that you read this book before we continue our monthly conversation, because we really need to be on the same page. My own sense of self has been shaken, and from this moment on, there may be only chaotic enthusiasm (or sociological neutrality) where there was once sensible and occasionally inspired recommendation. I may go and have a look at that Elmander goal again. It might help to ground me. You can still have good goals and bad goals, right? Right? *

MARCH/APRIL 2011

In April 2010, I was a tragic victim of the volcanic ash cloud that grounded all flights into, out of, and across Europe for a few days. I am sure that other people have hard-luck stories, too: weddings, births, and funerals were missed, job opportunities went begging, feckless husbands given one last chance got home to find their underwear strewn across the street, and so on. Mine, however, was perhaps more poignant than any of them: my family, stranded in Tenerife, was unable to celebrate my fifty-third birthday with me. Can you imagine? Of all the birthdays to miss, it had to be the one I was looking forward to the most. All my life I had wondered what it would be like to turn fifty-three, to open presents suitable for a fifty-three-year-old—something from the excellent Bald Guyz* range of beauty products, for example, or a Bruce Springsteen box set—while an adoring family looked on. Well, my adoring family was stranded on an island in the Mediterranean, in a hotel that apparently laid on a chocolate fountain for breakfast. When they eventually made it home, my birthday was clearly an event to be celebrated when it came around again in 2011, rather than retrospectively. I have therefore decided, perhaps understandably, that this April I will be turning fifty-three again. It's not a vanity thing; it's simply that I'm owed a birthday.

Back in 2010, I had to make do with the cards I'd been dealt, and the cards were these: a small group of friends bought me champagne, which we drank in my garden on a beautiful spring evening, at a time when I would usually be embarking on some terrible, strength-sapping, pointless fight about, say, shampoo and/or bedtime; the same friends then took me to a favorite local restaurant and gave me presents. You can see why I might feel bitter even to this day.

Three of the presents my friends had bought me were book-shaped, and, miraculously, given the lack of deferred gratification in my book-buying life, I wanted to read them all, and didn't own any of them. I got a lovely first edition of Mordecai Richler's *The Apprenticeship of Duddy Kravitz,* a copy of *Game Change: Obama and the Clintons, McCain and Palin, and the Race of a Lifetime* by John Heilemann and Mark Halperin, and Marc Norman's history of screenwriting, *What Happens Next.* Is it too late and too hurtful to say that my fifty-third birthday was perhaps the best ever?

Several months later, and I have finally read one of the three, even though I wanted to read all three of them immediately. (What happened in between? Other books, is what happened. Other books, other moods, other obligations, other appetites, other reading jour-

---

* Bald Guyz makes head wipes, moisturizing gel, and all kinds of great stuff for men who have chosen to live a hair-free life. The company has not paid for this endorsement, but I am very much hoping it will, or that it will send me a crate of free stuff.

neys.) *Game Change,* as you may or may not know, is about the 2008 election in the U.S., and appeared in a couple of the best-of-year lists here in the U.K., so I was reminded that I owned it; when I read it, I was reminded that politicians are unlike anyone I have ever met in my life.

Maybe some of you know politicians. Maybe you hang out with them, went to school with them, exchange Christmas cards with them. I'm guessing not, though. Politicians tend not to hang out with people like you, almost by definition. Typically, someone interested enough in the arts to be reading the *Believer* has spent a lot of time doing things that disqualify you not only from a career in politics, but from even knowing people who have a career in politics. While you were smoking weed, sleeping around, listening to Pavement, reading novels, watching old movies, and generally pissing away every educational opportunity ever given to you, they were knocking on doors, joining societies, reading the *Economist,* and being very, very careful about avoiding people and situations that might embarrass them later. They are the people who were knocking on your door five minutes after you arrived at college, asking for your vote in the forthcoming student-representative election; you thought they were creeps, and laughed at them behind their backs. Meanwhile, they thought you were unserious and unfocused, and patronized you irritatingly if you ever had cause to be in the same room. I hope that, however old you are, you have already done enough to kill any serious political ambition. If you haven't wasted huge chunks of your life on art, booze, and soft drugs, then you've wasted huge chunks of your life, and we don't want you around here. Go away.

Many of the characters in *Game Change* are quite clearly creeps. They are not portrayed as creeps, for the most part. John Heilemann and Mark Halperin obviously like the people who want to govern us, and their book, which is an unavoidable, enthralling mix of the gossipy and the profoundly significant, reflects this affection. And yet I defy anyone from around these parts to read this book without thinking, over and over again, Who are these people? There's John Edwards, of course, whose affair with the extraordinary Rielle Hunter was conducted more or less entirely in full view of an increasingly incredulous staff; when Edwards eventually realized the damage he had done to himself and his campaign, he lambasted a young staffer because he didn't come to his boss "like a fucking man and tell me to stop fucking her." But there are plenty of other strange people, too—people who don't really seem to believe anything, but who are desperately anxious to know what the country wants to hear them saying.

Obama is different, of course, but it's still very difficult to fathom why anyone would want to become a world leader. It's really not a nice job. For four hundred thousand dollars a year—plus a nineteen-thousand-dollar entertainment budget, although I would imagine very little of that can go on CDs, books, and cinema tickets—you give up safety, family life, social life, sleep, a significant proportion of your sanity, and the esteem of approximately two in every three of your fellow citizens. I am not being flippant: this is an intolerable prospect, for anyone with any sense of an inner life. This means that the people who want to represent us are actually the least representative people in the world.

Here in Europe, we still love Obama. But right at the beginning of *Game Change,* when Halperin and Heilemann are describing his relationship with Hillary Clinton, there is a line intended to convey how close the two were, once upon a time, but that serves only to make you wonder about politicians as a species. "At one point, Obama gave her a gift: a photograph of him, Michelle, and their two young daughters, Sasha and Malia." So, hold on… Hillary was Barack's mother? Because if she wasn't, why on earth would he give her a picture of himself and his kids? Would you do that with someone you knew professionally? "Here's a framed picture of me. Put it up anywhere in your house. It doesn't have to be on your mantelpiece. Or put it up in your office, on the half a shelf you have available for photos of your loved ones." Try it, and see how often you're invited to after-work drinks.

Game Change isn't the book I thought it would be, perhaps because the nomination race and the presidential campaign were not what they looked like from across the Atlantic. I was expecting a thrilling and inspirational story, full of goodies and baddies, dizzying highs and dispiriting lows; instead, Heilemann and Halperin describe a long, strength-sapping, and bitter trudge to victory. Much of the book is taken up with the inevitability of Clinton's defeat, and her refusal to acknowledge it, while Obama waits with weary impatience. And the fight between Obama and McCain is a nonevent once Sarah Palin joins in and makes the sides uneven. This is not to say that Game Change is dull. It isn't, because every page feels like the truth. It's just that the truth isn't as uplifting as you want to believe.

It was the holiday season here in the U.K., which explains the brevity of the Books Read list: my intellectual life is utterly dependent on my children attending school. The holiday season doesn't explain why I didn't pick up any fiction, nor does it explain why I should choose to spend all my available reading time on the unpromising subjects of American politics and cancer cells. I will only regret it if Game Change and The Immortal Life of Henrietta Lacks turn out to be the last two books I ever read, because I don't think they illustrate the breathtaking range of my literary tastes. They make me look like the kind of nonfiction guy I meet on planes during book tours. "Should I have heard of you? See, I don't read many novels. I like to learn something I didn't know already." At the time of writing I am halfway through a short and very beautiful YA novel, the completion of which should recomplicate me; meanwhile, you'll have to forgive these pages of the Believer temporarily resembling the books section of Business Traveller magazine.

Maybe the business travelers know what they're talking about, though, because The Immortal Life of Henrietta Lacks is riveting, beautifully written, and, yes, educational. I learned stuff. I learned so much stuff that I kept blurting it out to anyone who'd listen. Do you know who Henrietta Lacks was? Have you ever heard of the HeLa cells? Did you know that they can be found in just about any research lab in the world? And so on. I'll tell you, you don't want to be living with me at the moment. I'm even more boring than usual.

Rebecca Skloot's extraordinary book is the story of a dirt-poor black woman who died an agonizing death from cervical cancer in 1951. Just before Henrietta died, however, a surgeon sliced off a piece of her tumor and gave it to a research scientist called George Gey, who had been trying to grow human cells for years. Henrietta's cells, however, grew like kudzu, for reasons that are still not entirely clear to scientists; they grew so fast, so uncontrollably, that when you look up HeLa on Wikipedia, the entry uses the word *contamination* in the first four lines. HeLa is so powerful and fierce and durable, so eager to reproduce itself, that it gets into everything.

After I had read the first three or four chapters, I was a little worried on Skloot's behalf: I thought she was telling the story too quickly. Henrietta's cells were duplicating, her place in medical history was assured... maybe the last couple of hundred pages would turn out to be the first one hundred rehashed and analyzed, and the book would lose its breathtaking opening momentum. But the author knows what she has, and what she has is a gold mine of material dealing with class, race, family, science, and the law in America. In fact, *The Immortal Life of Henrietta Lacks,* like Adrian Nicole LeBlanc's incredible *Random Family,* is about pretty much everything. (*Random Family* and Skloot's book both took a decade to research and write, perhaps not coincidentally. I suspect that in both cases, the subject matter grew richer and richer with each year of contemplation.) Skloot tells brief, vivid, and astonishing stories of medical-ethics cases; she follows the cells as they get blasted into space and help find a vaccine for polio; she weaves in the lives of Henrietta's children as they struggle through the decades following their mother's death. They had no idea that she had achieved immortality until the 1970s, because nobody had ever taken the trouble to tell them, or to ask their permission—a courtesy denied Henrietta herself, of course. And while you can go online this very second and buy HeLa cells, the Lacks family has struggled, mostly in vain, for employment, access to health care, and recognition for Henrietta's contribution to science. If I come across a book as good, as gripping, as well constructed, and as surprising as this in the rest of 2011, I will be a happy and grateful man.

Contemporary fiction is OK, but you don't really learn anything from it, do you? It's mostly written by a bunch of arty losers who couldn't be bothered to go out and get a proper job, and who don't know anything about the world anyway. Nonfiction, that's the thing. Or historical fiction, because you know when you're reading it that people have done a whole load of research into nineteenth-century brick-making. Or thrillers, because you can learn a lot of things about high-grade weaponry. My New Year's resolution is to get a job as a, you know, a business guy, and join a business-guy book club. Plus, I'm going to befriend an important politician, a minister or a secretary of state. If any of you ministers or secretaries of state out there subscribe to this magazine and read this column, then face-book me, OK? I am literally holding my breath, so hurry. ✶

MAY 2011

I first and last read John Updike when I was in my twenties: I devoured all the *Rabbit* books that had been published at that point, and looked forward to a time in my life when I would be old enough to understand them. All that adultery and misery and ambition and guilt looked completely thrilling back then, but mystifying, too. Where did it all come from? And why, aged twenty-five, was I not grown up enough to be experiencing any of it? What was wrong with me? I suspect I didn't read any more of Updike's novels after that point simply because they made me feel inadequate, in ways that I hadn't previously considered. New forms of inadequacy I could live without, seeing as I didn't know what to do with the ones I was already aware of.

I'm not quite sure why an unread copy of *Marry Me* winked at me from my bookshelves just before I flew to the U.S. for a work trip recently. On the cover of the book, Paul Theroux promises us that "Updike has never written better of the woe that is marriage," but I can assure you (and my wife) that it wasn't the cheery blurb that lured me in. Perhaps I wanted to test myself again, a quarter of a century after the last time: had I got any closer to adulthood? Would I now, finally, be able to see a reflection of my own domestic circumstances?

"'You dumb cunt,' he said, and bounced her into the mattress again and again, 'you get a fucking grip on yourself. You got what you wanted, didn't you? This is it. Married bliss.'

"She spat in his face, *ptuh,* like a cat, a jump ahead of thought; saliva sprayed back down upon her own face and as it were awakened her…"

I am embarrassed to say that life is only very rarely like this *chez nous.* There's the holiday season, obviously, and the occasional Saturday night, especially during January and May, when, typically, my football team Arsenal crash out of the major competitions. But, hand on heart, I could not claim that we scale these particular giddy heights of seriousness with the kind of frequency that would allow me to gasp with recognition. I was even more cowed by the way this scene concludes, half a page and fourteen lines of dialogue later:

"'You're a nice man.' She hugged him, having suppressed a declaration of love.

"Wary, he wanted to sleep. 'Good night, sweetie.'"

I don't like to point the finger, and in any case my wife is generally a pacific and forgiving person. But the truth is that whenever I do call her the *c*-word and bounce her into the mattress again and again, she has never once told me that I'm "a nice man"—she tends to remain cross with me for hours. This means, in turn, that I have never been able to find it in myself to say "Good night, sweetie," and put the whole unfortunate episode behind us. In other words, it's her fault that we are not yet Updikean. She's a forty-five-year-old child.

It wasn't just the rows I found hard to comprehend; some of the sex was beyond me, too. "Though Sally had been married ten years, and furthermore had had lovers before Jerry, her lovemaking was wonderfully virginal, simple, and quick." Ah, yes. That's what we gentlemen want: women who are both sexually experienced and alive to the touch, while at the same time not too, you know, trampy. "Wonderfully virginal"? My therapist would have more fun in fifty minutes than he'd ever had in his whole professional life were I to use that particular combination of adverb and adjective in a session.

Marry Me was, as you can probably imagine, totally compelling, if extraordinarily dispiriting in its conviction that trying to extract the misery out of monogamy is like trying to extract grapes from wine. We worry a lot about how technology will date fiction; it had previously occurred to me that books written in the last quarter of the twentieth century would lead me to wonder whether something fundamental has changed in the relationships between men and women. I'm not sure we do feel that husbands and wives are doomed to suspicion, enmity, and contempt any longer, do we? Or am I making a twit of myself again? I suppose it's the latter. It usually is.

Worryingly—and this must remain completely between us— I recognized myself more frequently in the checklist Jon Ronson refers to in the title of his book than I did in *Marry Me*. (I'm not going to repeat the title. You'll have to go to the trouble of glancing up at the top of the previous page, and maybe you won't bother, and then you'll think better of me.) "Glibness/superficial charm"? Well, I have my moments, even if I do say so myself. And have you lost some weight? "Lack of realistic long-term goals"? I wouldn't call literary immortality unrealistic, exactly. It's more or less happened to Chaucer and Shakespeare, and I'm miles better than either of those. "Grandiose sense of self-worth"? Ah, now there at least I can plead not guilty. "Need for stimulation/

proneness to boredom"? I literally stopped in the middle of typing out that last sentence in order to play *Plants vs. Zombies,* although I did get bored of that after a couple of hours, so perhaps there is hope for me. "Poor behavioral controls"? Again, there is a glimmer of light, because I have just put out my last cigarette, and eaten my last biscuit.

Jon Ronson, as those of you who have read *Them* or *The Men Who Stare at Goats* will know, is a fearless nonfiction writer, so familiar with, and curious about, the deranged and the fanatical that he probably asks for his hair to be cut with a lunatic fringe. *Them* dealt with extremists of all hues, and *The Men Who Stare at Goats* was about that section of the American military who believe that one day wars might be won using mind-control and gloop. *The Psychopath Test,* as the title suggests, cuts straight to the chase.

It begins with a mystery: why were a group of academics, mostly neurologists, all sent a book by "Joe K" that consisted entirely of cryptic messages and holes? The perplexed neurologists believed that Ronson was the man to solve the puzzle, and their instincts were sound, because he does so. On the way, he meets a man who pretended to be mad in order to escape a prison sentence, and now cannot convince anybody that he is sane; several Scientologists engaged in a war on psychiatry, as Scientologists tend to be; Bob Hare, the man who devised the eponymous test; and a top CEO whose legendary ruthlessness leads Ronson to suspect that he might tick a few too many boxes. (It is Bob Hare's contention that psychopaths are all around us, in positions that allow them to exert and abuse their authority.) Like all Ronson's work, *The Psychopath Test* is funny, frightening, and provocative: it had never occurred to me, for example, that Scientologists had any kind of an argument for their apparently absurd war on science, but Ronson's account of the equally absurd experiments and treatments for which respected psychiatrists are responsible gives one pause for thought.

If you are a subscriber to this magazine, and a regular reader of this column, and you have very little going on in your life, and you're kind of anal, you may be thinking to yourself, Hey! It's eight weeks since he last wrote a column, and he's read exactly four books! There are various explanations and excuses I could give you, but the two most pertinent are as follows:

(1) I have been cruelly tricked into cofounding a writing center for kids, with a weird shop at the front of it, here in London (and don't even think about copying this idea in the U.S. unless you want to hear from our lawyers—although why you would want to spend a thousand hours and a million pounds a week doing so I can't imagine).

(2) I have spent way too much time watching the Dillon Panthers, the fictional football team at the heart of the brilliant drama series *Friday Night Lights.* (And yes, I know, I know—I have seen the fourth season. I am being respectful to those who are catching up.)

Reading time, in other words, has been in short supply, even during the day, and half the reading that has got done is directly related to the above. H. G. Bissinger's terrific nonfiction book, the source for a movie and then the TV series, is about the Permian Panthers, who represent a high school in Odessa, Texas, and regularly play in front of crowds of twenty thousand—or did, when the book was published in the early '90s. There is no equivalent of high-school or college football in Europe, for several reasons: there are no comparable sports scholarships, for a start, and, in a country the size of England, it's quite hard to live more than fifty miles from a pro team. And in any case, because your major sports have turned out to be so uninteresting to the rest of the world, young talent in the U.S. is governable; the young soccer players of London and Manchester no longer compete with each other for a place in a top professional team, but with kids from Africa and Asia and Spain. Over the last several years, Arsenal has routinely played without a single English player in their starting eleven. Our best player is Spanish; one of our brightest hopes for the future is Japanese and currently on loan to a club in Holland. So the idea of an entire community's aspirations being embodied in local teen-age athletes is weird, but not unappealing.

The reality, as Bissinger presents it—and he went to live in Odessa for a year, hung out with players and coaching staff and fans, so he knows what he's talking about—is a lot darker, however. It turns out that there are not as many liberals in small-town Texas as the TV series would have me believe: in Dillon, people are always speaking out against racism, or talking about art, or thinking about great literature. (The adorably nerdy Landry Clarke can quite clearly be seen reading *High Fidelity,* my first novel, in an episode of the third season. This is almost certainly the greatest achievement of my writing career. And I'm sorry to bring it up, but I had to tell somebody.) In Odessa, Dillon's real-life counterpart... not so much racism gets confronted, or towering masterpieces of fiction consumed. Bissinger loves his football, and falls in love with the team, but is powerfully good on what the town's obsession with football costs its kids. It's not just the ones who don't make it, or become damaged along the way, all of whom get chucked away like ribs stripped of their meat (and catastrophically uneducated before they've been rejected); the kids who can't play football are almost worthless. The girls spend half their time cheerleading and cake-baking for the players, and the students with more cerebral interests are ignored. In the season that Bissinger followed the team, the cost of rush-delivered postgame videotapes that enabled the coaches to analyze what had gone right and wrong was $6,400. The budget for the entire English department was $5,040. And the team used private jets for away games on more than one occasion. Isn't it great how little you need to spend to inculcate a passion for the arts? Perhaps I have drawn the wrong conclusion.

David Almond's *My Name Is Mina* is an extraordinary children's book by the author of *Skellig,* one of the best novels written for anyone published in the last fifteen years. And this new book is a companion piece to *Skellig,* a kind of prequel about the girl who lives next door. It's also, as it turns out, a handbook for anyone who is in-

terested in literacy and education as they have been, or are being, ap-
plied to them or their children or anybody else's children:

> Why should I write something so that somebody could say I was
> well below average, below average, average, above average, or well
> above average? What's average? And what about the ones that find
> out they're well below average? What's the point of that and how's
> that going to make them feel for the rest of their lives? And did
> William Blake do writing tasks just because somebody else told him
> to? And what Level would he have got anyway?

> "Little Lamb, Who mad'st thee?
> Dost thou know who mad'st thee?"

> What level is that?

Almond's wry disdain for the way we sift our children as if they
were potatoes killed me, because I was once found to be below average, across the board, at a crucial early stage in my educational career, and I have just about recovered enough confidence to declare
that this judgment was, if not wrong, then at least not worth making. I think that, like everybody, I'm above average at some things
and well below at others.

My Name Is Mina is a literary novel for kids, a Blakean mys-
tic's view of the world, a fun-filled activity book for a rainy day
("EXTRAORDINARY ACTIVITY—Write a poem that repeats
a word and repeats a word and repeats a word and repeats a word
until it almost loses its meaning"), a study of loneliness and grief,
and it made more sense to me than half the fiction I usually read.
This can't be right, and I won't allow it to be right. For literary
purposes only, I am off to call my wife obscenities and bounce her
up and down on a mattress. As I write, she's upstairs, helping my
youngest son with his homework, so she's in for a shock. ✶

JUNE 2011

My friendship with the writer Sarah Vowell— history buff, TV and radio personality, occasional animated character—is now fifteen years old. For the first decade or so, it was pretty straightforward: whenever I was in New York, we would sit in a park staring at a statue of an obscure but allegedly important American figure, and she would talk about it while I nodded and smoked. Over the last few years, however, it has become complicated to the extent that it has started to resemble one of those Greek myths where the hero (in this case, me) is asked to perform tasks by some enigmatic and implacable goddess (her) or monster (also her). Vowell isn't as well known in the U.K. as she should be—we have different chat shows, for a start, and because of the awesomely uncompromising insularity of her writing, her books aren't published here. So, as one of her few English fans, I have been taking the literary challenges that she throws across the Atlantic personally. In my mind, at least, it goes like this. I tell her that I am an enormous admirer of her work, and she says, "In that case, I am going to write a book about the museums of the assassinated American presidents, excluding the most recent, and therefore the only one you are interested in. Will you read it?" I read it, loved it, told her so.

"I see that you are a worthy English opponent, so I will have to try harder. I will now make you read a book about New England Puritans—not the Plymouth Pilgrims, but the more obscure (and more self-denying) Massachusetts Bay crowd." I read it, loved it, asked her to hit me with something a little less accessible.

And now she has come roaring back with *Unfamiliar Fishes,* a history of Hawaii, although obviously it's not a complete history of Hawaii, because a complete history of Hawaii would not have intimidated the English reader to quite the required extent, and might have contained some fun facts about Bette Midler. Vowell wisely chose to concentrate on the nineteenth century, post-1820, when her old friends from New England sailed around the entire American continent in order to tell the natives that everything they had hitherto believed was wrong. (One of the many things I had never thought about before reading *Unfamiliar Fishes* was the sheer uselessness of New England as a home base for missionaries. It took them a good six months to get to anywhere uncivilized enough to need them.)

Unfamiliar Fishes tells the story of the battle for hearts and minds between the Massachusetts killjoys and the locals. In these wars, the liberal conscience always has us rooting for the locals, even though we invariably already know that we are doomed to disappointment, and that the locals, whoever and wherever they might be, are even as we speak tucking into Happy Meals, listening to Adele, and working for Halliburton. In Hawaii, though, there was a lot invested in the idea that a child born from the union between brother and sister was superior to a child conceived any other way, and this particular belief kind of muddied the water a little for me. I know, I know. Different times, different cultures. But I have a sister, and you too may well have a sibling who operates an entirely different genital system. And if you do, then you might find yourself unable to boo the meddling Christians with the volume you can usually achieve in situations like this.

And yet as Vowell points out, the whole foundation of royalty is based on the notion that one bloodline is superior to another, and therefore shouldn't be messed with. "The way said contamination is prevented is through inbreeding, which, of course, is often the genetic cause of a royal dynasty's demise through sterility, miscarriages, stillbirths, and sickliness. That would be true of the heirs of Keopuolani just as it was true of the House of Hapsburg."

In other words, one of the reasons that my own country is in such a mess is that there simply hasn't been enough in-breeding: if there had, we might be shot of our Royal Family by now. Incest is more complicated than it looks (and please feel free to go and get that printed on a T-shirt, if it's a slogan that grabs you). Like anything else, it's got its good points and its bad.

The one team we can all get behind in *Unfamiliar Fishes* is the crew of the English whaler *John Palmer.* They were so annoyed by the missionaries messing with their inalienable right to onboard visits from prostitutes that they started shelling the port. I am, however, grudgingly respectful of the Americans who, convinced of the Hawaiians' need for a Bible, first helped to invent a written Hawaiian language, and then translated the whole thing from the original Greek and Hebrew. It took them seventeen years. Finally I have a notion of what I might do when I retire. Anyway, I have sailed through yet another task set by the dark nerd-maiden from across the water; I don't think she is capable of writing anything that I wouldn't read, although I hope she doesn't take that as a provocation. And her history of whaling on the island was so enthralling that it got me through the entire first chapter of *Moby-Dick*.

The idea of this column, for those of you who have arrived eight years late, is that I write about what I have read in the previous month; for some reason, the books I read with my children have never been included. This last couple of months, however, we have been reading Andy Stanton's *Mr. Gum* series at bedtime, and as Stanton's books are providing as much joy to me as they do to the boys, their omission from these pages would be indefensible.

Mr. Gum is an evil, joyless, smelly old man who tries to poison dogs, and whose favorite TV program is *Bag of Sticks,* which is as exciting as it sounds. His best friend is the evil butcher Billy William the Third, and his enemies are the entirely admirable Polly, Friday O'Leary, and the billionaire gingerbread man with electric muscles, little Alan Taylor. The books are a happy product of a tolerably nonincestuous relationship between Roald Dahl and Monty Python, and they are properly funny: Stanton has an eccentric imagination, and an anarchic verbal wit that occasionally redirects his narrative in directions that possibly even the author didn't expect.

My sons' enormous enjoyment of the books has been intensified through a series of superb readings by their father, readings that, in his mind at least, are comparable only to the performances Dickens is reported to have given at public events. Billy William the Third is rendered as an evil version of the great English comic actor Kenneth Williams, Alan Taylor as the football commentator John Motson, and Mr. Gum as a kind of ancient Cockney gangster paterfamilias. It seems ridiculous that performances with this level of invention take place night after night in a child's bedroom, in front of an audience of two; I may well have to throw them open to the public.

If you, like me, have been cursed by boy-children, you too may have found that their relationship with books is a fractious one, no matter how many times they see a male role model lounging around the house with his nose glued to a partial history of

Hawaii. Andy Stanton's series has been a real breakthrough, and a testament to the importance and the power of jokes; we are just about to start the seventh of the eight books, and I'm already fearful of the Gumless future.

I don't have the heart to tell my sons that the older one gets, the less funny literature becomes—and they would refuse to believe me if I tried to explain that some people don't think jokes even belong in proper books. I won't bother breaking the news that, if they remain readers, they will insist on depressing themselves for about a decade of their lives, in a concerted search for gravitas through literature. Charles Portis is a *Believer* favorite (one of our editors wrote an enormous and completely excellent piece about him in the very early days of this magazine's life) partly because he takes his humor seriously: the Coen brothers' recent adaptation of *True Grit* was admirable in many ways, but it didn't really convey the comic brilliance of the novel, nor was it able to, as so much of it was embedded in the voice of the priggish, god-fearing Mattie Ross. I suspect that we have the Coen brothers to thank for the reappearance of Portis's first novel, *Norwood,* in bookstores, so they have done their bit for comedy anyway.

"Norwood" is Norwood Pratt, a marine who obtains a hardship discharge so that he can return to Texas to look after his incapable sister Vernell. Vernell promptly marries an unlikable disabled veteran called Bill Bird, however, thus liberating Norwood to go to New York, partly in an attempt to reclaim seventy dollars that an army friend owes him. So *Norwood* is a road-trip book, and the simplicity of its structure allows for a dazzling range of eccentric minor characters, and plenty of room for any number of terrific, short, often crazily pointless passages of dialogue. Here's Norwood, on a bus, trying to engage with a two-year-old called Hershel Remley:

> "I believe the cat has got that boy's tongue," said Norwood.
> "Say no he ain't," said Mrs. Remley. "Say I can talk aplenty when I want to, Mr. Man."

"Tell me what your name is," said Norwood. "What is your name?"

"Say Hershel. Say Hershel Remley is my name."

"How old are you, Hershel? Tell me how old you are."

"Say I'm two years old."

"Hold up this many fingers," said Norwood.

"He don't know about that," said Mrs. Remley. "But he can blow out a match."

There's so much to love here: the portrayal of the clearly slow-witted toddler, Mrs. Remley's desperate and hopeful pride, the author's merciless ear for disastrous parental anthropomorphizing... This is the third novel I have read by Charles Portis, and I am now completely convinced that he's a neglected comic genius. And here's a cool fact: in Nora Ephron's new book of essays, *I Remember Nothing,* she talks about dating Portis in the '60s. The relationship clearly didn't last, but it feels as though their children are everywhere anyway.

Tom Rachman's *The Imperfectionists,* which I suspect you may have read already, is an ingeniously structured work of fiction that manages to tell the entire history of an English-language newspaper based in Rome through a series of linked short stories about its members of staff. This to me makes *The Imperfectionists* a collection rather than a novel, despite the bald assertion on the cover ("A Novel"), and I slightly resented being misled, for entirely indefensible reasons; in most ways I haven't aged at all over the last quarter of a century, remarkably, but I seemed to have developed some kind of old-geezerish resentment of story collections. Is that possible? Is resentment of short fiction a sign of aging, like liver spots? And if it is, then why? As the end of one's life draws closer, surely one should embrace short fiction, not spurn it. And yet I was extremely conscious of not wanting to make the emotional effort at the beginning of each chapter, to the extent that I could almost hear myself grumbling like my grandmother used to. "Who are these people, now? I don't know them.

Where did the other ones go? They'd only just got here." It's a great tribute to Rachman, to his sense of pace and his choice of narrative moment, that within a couple of pages I had forgiven him. And the world of the expatriate is, it occurred to me halfway through the book, rich with fictional possibilities; almost by definition, the characters are lost, restless, discontented—just the way we like them.

I feel that I cannot leave before explaining some of the more baffling choices in the Books Bought column. Lawrence W. Levine's *Highbrow/Lowbrow* was, along with John Seabrook's *Nobrow,* a recommendation from a reader who felt it might help me with some of the difficult issues raised by Carl Wilson's essay on Céline Dion; the book about Ronald Reagan's time at General Electric I bought after watching a riveting Reagan documentary on the BBC. The chances of me reading either of them are, I suspect, slim; as is so often the case, however, I am, at relatively modest expense, intent on maintaining a risible self-delusion about my intellectual curiosity. I know way too much about James Brown already, so I'll probably choose that one next. ✱

JULY/AUGUST 2011

BOOKS BOUGHT:
* *Mrs. Caliban*— Rachel Ingalls
* *Whoops!: Why Everyone Owes Everyone and No One Can Pay*— John Lanchester
* *Adventures of Huckleberry Finn*— Mark Twain
* *The Writer's Journey: Mythic Structure for Writers*—Christopher Vogler

BOOKS READ:
* *Sum: Forty Tales from the Afterlives*— David Eagleman
* *Ball of Fire: The Tumultuous Life and Comic Art of Lucille Ball*—Stefan Kanfer
* *Nothing to Envy: Ordinary Lives in North Korea*—Barbara Demick
* *Whoops!: Why Everyone Owes Everyone and No One Can Pay*— John Lanchester
* *Adventures of Huckleberry Finn*—Mark Twain

No time spent with a book is ever entirely wasted, even if the experience is not a happy one: there's always something to be learned. It's just that, every now and again, you can hit a patch of reading that makes you feel as if you're pootling about. There's nothing like a couple of sleepy novels, followed by a moderately engaging biography of a minor cultural figure, to make you aware of your own mortality. But what can you do about it? We don't choose to waste our reading time; it just happens. The books let us down.

It wasn't just that I enjoyed all the books I read this month; they felt vital, too. If you must read a biography of a sitcom star, then make sure the sitcom is the most successful and influential in TV history. You have a yen to read about a grotesquely dysfunctional communist society? Well, don't mess about with Cuba—go straight for North Korea. John Lanchester's *Whoops!* is a relatively simple explanation of the biggest financial crisis in history; Mark Twain's *Adventures of Huckleberry Finn* is, according to Hemingway, the book from which all American literature derives. A month of superlatives, in other words—the best, the worst, the biggest, and the most important.

And, as a digestif, David Eagleman's *Sum,* which invites us to contemplate forty varieties of afterlife. It's such a complete package that it seems crazy to carry on reading, so I may well stop altogether. I'm not giving this column up, though. It pays too well.

Stefan Kanfer's *Ball of Fire* contains an anecdote which seems to me to justify not only the time I spent reading it, but the entire genre, every biography ever written. Kanfer is describing the early days of Ball's relationship with Desi Arnaz, which was stormy right from the off:

> Almost every Sunday night ended with a furious argument about each other's intentions and infidelities... It happened that two of the town's greatest magpies witnessed many of the quarrels. F. Scott Fitzgerald and his inamorata, columnist Sheilah Graham, used to watch the spats from Fitzgerald's balcony.

F. Scott Fitzgerald used to watch Lucille Ball and Desi Arnaz fighting? Why didn't I know this before? If this story is true—and there's no reason to doubt it—then all is chaos. No biography can be left unread, just in case there is a gem like this lying there, undiscovered, within its pages. Maybe Thomas Pynchon repeatedly bangs on Sarah Michelle Gellar's wall because she plays her music too loud! Maybe Simon Cowell and Maya Angelou are in the same book group!

The reason Kanfer's book works so well, and why it throws up so many good stories, is that Ball, like the fictional Mose Sharp and Rocky Carter in Elizabeth McCracken's brilliant *Niagara Falls All Over Again,* took the long road through the American pop-culture century. She worked in theater, film, radio, and TV. She dated Henry Fonda, worked with the Marx Brothers, knew Damon Runyon. A washed-up Buster Keaton helped her with her physical comedy. She found out that she was pregnant by listening to Walter Winchell on the radio—he'd obtained the information from the lab technicians even before they passed the information on to Ball's doctor. She attracted the attention of HUAC, the House Un-American Activities Committee, because she'd registered with the Communist party in 1936 primarily to humor her socialist grandfather. Hers was an extraordinary journey, and just in case you need a little more, there was a long, tempestuous marriage at the center of it. (Ball rendered the first divorce from Arnaz null and void by jumping into bed with her ex-husband on the way back from the courthouse.) We didn't have a Lucille Ball in the U.K.; you have way more female comediennes than us. This is not a coincidence.

There wasn't any logic behind my decision to go straight from *Ball of Fire* to the banking crisis, although John Lanchester's *Whoops!* (published in the U.S. as *I.O.U.*) certainly bolstered the sense of elegiac melancholy that lingers after you've said goodbye to Lucy and Desi and the Golden Age of Television. We now have more to worry about than the end of wholesome, nation-uniting family sitcoms; it turns out that the Golden Age of Everything is over. One of Lanchester's contentions is that "Western liberal democracies are the best societies that have ever existed… Citizens of those societies are, on aggregate, the most fortunate people who have ever lived." I'll be comparing and contrasting with North Korea a little later, but when you consider that one of the indicators of poverty in the U.S. and the U.K. is obesity, you can see his point. Nobody is obese in North Korea.

Now, however, the citizens of the U.S. and the U.K. have some bills to pay. One authoritative market commentator puts the cost of the bailout in the U.S. at just over $4.5 trillion—a number "bigger than the Marshall Plan, the Louisiana Purchase, the Apollo moon landings, the 1980s savings and loan crisis, the Korean War, the New Deal, the invasion of Iraq, the Vietnam War, and the total cost of NASA's space flights, all added together—repeat, added together (and yes, the old figures are adjusted upward for inflation)." If you were thinking of knocking on the door of a government body because you're looking for a little help with your video installation... well, I'd give it a few weeks. Here in the U.K., the government is looking to make an unprecedented and almost certainly unachievable 25 percent cut in public services; we need to find in the region of £40 billion a year simply to service our debts.

There are plenty of numbers in *Whoops!* Most of them are scary, but some are funny, if your taste in humor leans toward the apocalyptic. In a brilliant chapter about the catastrophic failure of the mathematical models of risk used by bankers and economists, a chapter entitled The Mistake, Lanchester introduces us—well, me, anyway—to the notion of the sigma, a measure of probability. "A '3-sigma event' is something supposed to happen only 0.3 percent of the time, i.e., about once every three thousand times something is measured." According to the mathematical models, the 1987 Black Monday crash was a 10-sigma event; this means that, were the life of the universe repeated 1 billion times, it still shouldn't have happened. And yet it did. During the recent crash, the CFO of Goldman Sachs claimed that he was seeing twenty-five sigma events "*several days in a row.*" (My italics, but I'm sure I'm italicizing for all of us.) Lanchester tries to give us some sense of the numbers involved here, but it's basically hopeless: "Twenty sigma is ten times the number of all the particles in the known universe; 25-sigma is the same but with the decimal point moved fifty-two places to the right." Even if we presume that there are three particles in the known universe—

and I'm no physicist, but I'm guessing that three is probably on the low side—then the number is still impossible to grasp. And these people saw events on this scale of incomprehensible improbability happening every day for a week. They would presumably also have been staggered by Brazil winning the next World Cup, on the basis that they didn't win it yesterday or the day before or on any of the four and a half thousand days since their last victory, in 2002. (For those of you who don't follow soccer: Brazil are quite good. They always have a decent chance of winning the World Cup. But the World Cup takes place only every four years, so... Oh, forget it.) Meanwhile, the reality underpinning the numbers and the credit swaps and the securitization was a whole bunch of people who had been persuaded to take out mortgages that they couldn't afford, and had to pay more for them than people with a credit history and a job, because they were riskier. One thing that had never quite sunk in for me is that, for Wall Street and the City, subprime mortgages and junk bonds are Good Things—or used to be, anyway—so it wasn't as though the unscrupulous were hiding shoddy goods under the more-attractive stuff. The shoddy goods were attractive, and they wanted in. The higher the risk, the more money you make. Lovely. And the bankers thought they'd fixed it so that this risk had no downside, ever, for anyone. Securitization and its trimmings were, almost literally, alchemy, as far as the banks could tell.

One of the reasons *Whoops!* has done well in the U.K. is that John Lanchester is One of Us. He's not a financial journalist; he's a novelist, and a critic, and an outsider when it comes to this stuff. His dad was a bank manager, though, and he has the necessary interest, and the necessary anxiety. I watched *Inside Job* this month, too, and between them, Lanchester and Charles Ferguson have achieved the impossible, and made me feel... not knowledgeable, exactly, but at least I can see the dim light of comprehension breaking somewhere over the horizon. I don't know you personally, but I'm sort of presuming that you know more about the Decemberists and Jennifer Egan than you do about Gaussian copula formulas. Is that right? If so, then this is the book for you.

Nothing to Envy is a book about what happens when an economy fails completely, to the extent that there is nothing left—no work, no infrastructure, no food, no anything. I bought it after a forceful recommendation from a friend, and after it won a nonfiction prize in the U.K., and I wasn't sure I'd ever read it. But on the very first page there is a startling satellite picture of the Korean peninsula, taken at night, and I was hooked in. In this picture, the South looks like the U.S. or the U.K. or just about any twenty-first-century country, mottled with light from its cities, and great puddles of the stuff in the area around Seoul. In the North, it looks as though someone has a single candle burning in the capital, Pyongyang. Much of North Korea has no electricity. It's packed up. It went sometime in the early '90s, and it never came back. Sometimes—typically on the birthday of the Great Leader—it wheezes back into life for an hour or two, but the rest of the time North Korea is lost in a blackness of its own making.

Barbara Demick has pieced together a picture of daily life in this poor benighted country from the testimonies of people who got out. They weren't dissidents, because dissidence doesn't really exist in North Korea. How can it, when its citizens have never been presented with an alternative way of thinking, and when they have no access to books, magazines, newspapers, movies, TV, music, or ideas from any other part of the world? Even conversation is dangerous, when you have no way of knowing whether your friends, neighbors, even children are informants. You don't have a telephone, and you can't write to anyone when you have no pen or paper, and even if you do, the postman may well burn your letters simply because there's nothing else to burn. Meanwhile, everyone is starving to death. (Much of the book is about life in the 1990s, but, as Demick's epilogue and the most cursory Google search makes clear, nothing much has changed.) One of Demick's interviewees was a kindergarten teacher who saw her class go from fifty to fifteen kids. There is literally nothing to eat; they're peeling the bark off trees and boiling it up for soup. This is a country whose inhabitants have literally shrunk, while the rest of the world has got taller: the average North Korean seventeen-year-old boy is five inches smaller than his counterpart in the South.

A review quoted on my paperback edition tells us that this book is "required reading for anyone interested in the Korean peninsula"; I've just spent a few hundred words telling you how harrowing much of it is. We're not selling it to you, I can tell. And yet *Nothing to Envy* does have resonance, and it does transcend its subject matter, if that's what you want it to do. Both *Whoops!* and *Nothing to Envy* make it clear just how utterly dependent we all are on systems; without them, our much-cherished quirky individuality and our sense of moral self mean nothing. And I know this sounds weird and possibly callous, but Demick's book was every bit as absorbing as *Ball of Fire:* both contain a multitude of extraordinary stories, stories you want to remember. In other words, there is a kind of pleasure to be gained from the pain of others. That's the trouble with good writers. Only the bad ones make you want to do the human thing and look away.

I have almost no room to talk about *Sum* or *Huckleberry Finn.* Briefly: *Sum* I enjoyed, although I wish it had come with instructions. Was I supposed to read all the forty essays in one lump, which is what I did? Or was I supposed to pepper my month with them, treat myself to a tiny contemplation of what the afterlife is or does or should be at odd moments of the day and night? I suspect the latter. I blew it. As for *Huckleberry Finn,* the most important novel in American literature: Meh. That Tom Sawyer is a pill, isn't he? ✶

SEPTEMBER 2011

I know that you are younger than me, because more or less everyone is, nowadays. I am presuming, too, that if you have turned to this page of the *Believer* then you have an interest in books, and that if you read any of the rest of the magazine, then you are likely to have a deep passion for other forms of art. It is not too much of a stretch, then, to deduce from this information that your sexual relationships are complicated, morally dubious, and almost certainly unsavory, and I say that with as much neutrality as I can muster. So before I write about *Mating in Captivity,* Esther Perel's book about monogamous sex, I suppose I should clarify a couple of points for you.

Firstly: monogamy is this thing where you sleep with only one person. And I'm not talking about only one person during the whole length of Bonnaroo, or an art-film screening, or a poetry "happening," or whatever. Sometimes the commitment might last weeks, months even. (Married readers: in next month's column, I may introduce some more information, although I suspect they're some years away from being able to handle the dismal truth.) Esther Perel has cleverly recognized that a tiny minority of monogamists can occasionally feel a twinge of inexplicable and indefinable dissatisfaction with their chosen path—nothing significant, and certainly nothing that leads them to rethink their decision (monogamous relationships almost never fail, unless either partner is still sexually active)—and she has written a book that might help them through this tricky time. It's a niche market, obviously, the sexual equivalent of a guide for people whose pets have an alcohol-abuse problem. It's great that someone has done it, but it's not for everyone.

Secondly, I should also explain that I read this book for professional reasons, and professional reasons alone: I'm trying to write something about monogamy, god help me. I know that sounds dubious, but maybe you will believe me if I confess that my own marital problems lie beyond the reach of any self-help book available in a bookstore, or even on Amazon. They also lie beyond the reach of pills and tears, but perhaps I have said too much.

Mating in Captivity is a very wise book—I was going to say "surprisingly wise," because I have hitherto maintained the lit-snob assumption that nonfiction books that purport to improve your unhappy marriage or your failing career or your sickly spiritual well-being will actually do no such thing. (As we know around these parts, only Great Literature can save your soul, which is why all English professors are morally unimpeachable human beings, completely free from vanity, envy, sloth, lust, and so on.) Perel is very good on how the space between couples in which eroticism thrives, a space we are desperate to fill in the early days of a relationship, can be shrunk by domesticity and knowledge; there is a pragmatic understanding in her writing that is entirely winning and sympathetic.

She also has interesting things to say about the contemporary insistence that all intimacy is verbal intimacy, a cultural diktat that confuses and intimidates the kind of male whose inability to talk is then misinterpreted as an inability to commit, or a macho fear of weakness. Perel tells the rather sweet story of Eddie and Noriko, who literally couldn't communicate because they didn't speak the same language; Eddie had been ditched by scores of women who were impatient with his apparent unwillingness to bare his soul. "I really think that not being able to talk made this whole thing possible," Eddie tells Perel, twelve years into his marriage. "For once, there was no pressure on me to share. And so Noriko and I had to show how much we liked each other in other ways. We cooked for each other a lot, gave each other baths… It's not like we didn't communicate; we just didn't talk." MORE BATHS, LESS TALKING… If you're a woman who is currently and unhappily single, you could do a lot worse than put that slogan on a banner and march up and down your street.

"Some of America's best features—the belief in democracy, equality, consensus-building, compromise, fairness, and mutual tolerance—can, when carried too punctiliously into the bedroom, result in very boring sex," Perel says in a chapter entitled Democracy Versus Hot Sex. At the time of writing, Michele Bachmann has just announced her candidacy for the presidency, and another assumption I have made about you is that very few of you vote Republican. I don't think Esther Perel is encouraging you to do so, although if the unthinkable happens and Bachmann wins, there may well be some consolations, from the sound of it. (None of this applies to the British, of course, who live in a class-ridden monarchy, and as a consequence have hot sex every single day of their lives.)

My only complaint about this engaging and thoughtful book is that its author uses the word *vanilla* pejoratively too often, as a synonym for *bland, dull, safe*. This usage, I think, must stem from vanilla ice cream, which, typically, tastes of nothing and is certainly the unthinkable option if you're in an ice-cream establishment that offers scores of varieties. The flavor of the vanilla pod itself, however, is sophisticated, seductive, subtle. Have you tried the Body Shop Vanilla Shower Gel? I don't want to write advertising copy for multinational companies—not for free, anyway—but Body Shop Vanilla, it seems to me, is much more suggestive of deviance and light bondage than it is of the missionary position. And, guys, if you use that, could you credit the *Believer*? And also chuck them a few quid? Thanks.

I bought a couple of the books on the lists above after coming across a top-five that Woody Allen put together for the *Guardian*. I had never heard of Machado de Assis, and I probably wouldn't have thought of reading a biography of Elia Kazan had it not been for Allen's recommendation, but Richard Schickel's book chimed with the mood created by *Ball of Fire,* Stefan Kanfer's terrifically entertaining book about Lucille Ball, which I read recently.

Kazan, as you may or may not know, was the brilliant director of *On the Waterfront* and *A Streetcar Named Desire.* But he is now remembered almost as clearly because he chose to testify against former colleagues in front of the House Un-American Activities Committee (HUAC)—in 1952. Schickel begins his book, electrifyingly and provocatively, by coming out swinging on Kazan's behalf. I had never come across anyone attempting to do this before, and as a consequence I had always presumed that those who named names could safely be written off; god knows there are few enough examples of moral choices that are straightforwardly good or bad, and I had always valued the decision of Kazan and others as one of those that one didn't have to think about: they were wrong, full stop, and we are thus free to condemn them as viciously and as cheerfully as we want.

Yes, well. It turns out that it wasn't quite like that. Schickel's arguments are complicated and detailed, and I don't have the space to do them justice here, but then, complication and detail are precisely what have been lacking ever since the 1950s. Schickel describes the campaign against Kazan as "a typical Stalinist tactic— seize the high, easy-to-understand moral ground, then try to crush nuanced opposition to that position through simplifying sloganeering." I suspect that I'm not the only one who liked the look of that easy-to-understand moral ground, and there is a part of me that is actually irritated to discover that it's not as comfortable as it appeared. Schickel's jabs at the kidney—if that is where our fuzzy sense of morality is stored—are telling and sharp: naming names would have been fine if the names named had belonged to the Ku Klux Klan or the Nazi Party; there were lots of other, more-democratic leftist organizations that liberals could have signed up for; there were public protests against the Gulags as early as 1931, and there was really no excuse for those who defended Stalin in the 1950s; much of the outrage directed against Kazan was entirely synthetic. Rod Steiger, who appeared in *On the Waterfront* and was loudly and angrily opposed to the idea of Kazan receiving an honorary Oscar in 1999, told a reporter from *Time* that Kazan "was our father and he fucked us"; Schickel points out that the fucking was done well over a year before *On the Waterfront* started shooting—in other words, Steiger's moral objections came to the surface painfully slowly, and well after one of the most celebrated performances of his film career was safely in the can.

It was Dalton Trumbo, one of the writers blacklisted as a result of HUAC, who ended up making the best case for Kazan. The kind of person who testified, he said, was "a man who has left the CP to avoid constant attempts to meddle with the ideological content of his writing… a person whose disagreement with the CP had turned to forthright hostility and who, when the crunch came, saw no reason to sacrifice his career in defence of the rights of people he now hated…" All I want is one simple article of faith that is even less complicated than it looks. Is that too much to ask?

NICK HORNBY

There is a lot more to Kazan than all this, of course. He directed
the first production of *Death of a Salesman,* as well as the stage version of *A Streetcar Named Desire,* worked with Arthur Miller on several other occasions, slept with Monroe and Vivien Leigh, made *East
of Eden,* and wrote a novel that sold four million copies in the U.S.—
Kazan had a pretty impressive twentieth century. I wish Schickel's
book had been just that little bit more gossipy, not just because gos-
sip is fun, but because Kazan's relentless womanizing, it seems to me,
needed some kind of explanation or context. Schickel's refusal to
discuss Kazan's domestic arrangements seems indulgent, rather than
high-minded; Kazan is given a guys-will-be-guys (or, perhaps, great-
artists-will-be-great-artists) free pass that I don't think anyone ever
really earns. From the index: "Kazan, Molly Day Thacher (first wife)
husband's affairs and, 94–95, 388–89, 404." They were married for
thirty years.

Philip Roth was recently quoted as saying that he doesn't read
fiction anymore. "I wised up," he told an interviewer in the *Financial Times.* We all have moments like this: I have vowed, at various
points, never to read any more novels, and books about sport, and
thrillers where kids get murdered, and music biographies; but none
of these decisions ever holds for very long. Moods change, tastes re-
assert themselves, and a great book always shakes off its genre and
its subject matter anyway, although I fear that the desire to read
about the dismemberment of children and young women may have
left me forever. I'm not sure wisdom has much to do with any of
this, and I'd hate for Roth's words to be given extra weight just because of his age, his accomplishments, and the veneration he inspires.
I don't know if it's ever very wise to give up on Dickens. In my experience, a sudden panic about my own ignorance is followed firstly
by the desperate desire to read nonfiction, and then, usually very
swiftly, by a realization that any nonfiction reading I do is going to
be hopelessly inadequate and partial. If I knew I was going to die
next week, then I'd definitely be keen to read up on facts about the

afterlife; in the absence of any really authoritative books on this subject, however (no recommendations, please), then I think I'd rather read great fiction, something that shoots for and maybe even hits the moon, than a history of the House of Bourbon.

It is, perhaps, a little unfair to ask Eleanor Henderson to provide a philosophical justification for an entire art form, especially as *Ten Thousand Saints* is her first novel, but she does a pretty good job anyway. She moves in extraordinarily close to her young protagonists, participants in the New York straight-edge punk scene of the 1980s, and in doing so taught me a lot of things I didn't know. (Straight-edge was never much of a thing in England, where sobriety is seen as a moral failing by all ages and tribes.) The big draw here, though, is Henderson's writing, which is warm, engaged, and precise; I don't think I have ever come across a gritty urban novel that is as uninterested in finding a prose style to complement its subject. That's a good thing, by the way. *Ten Thousand Saints* is the offspring of Lester Bangs and Anne Tyler, and who wouldn't want to read that baby?

Per Petterson's beautiful, truthful *Out Stealing Horses* seems to me a pretty good example of the sort of thing that nonfiction can never accomplish. It's about aging and childhood, memory and family, and it has things to say on these subjects. That Petterson can accomplish this while providing an ornate, time-shifting narrative that includes—spoiler alert and hopeless volte-face, all at the same time—dead children seems to me the reason why we should never stop reading novels, however old and wise we are. ✶

OCTOBER 2011

I t is August, and as I write, burned-out buildings in London and other British cities are being demolished after several nights of astonishing and disturbing lawlessness. Meanwhile I am in the Dorset village of Burton Bradstock, listening to the sound of the wind-whipped sea smashing onto the shore, and to the young daughter of a friend playing "Chopsticks" over and over and over again on the piano belonging to the cliff-top house we have rented. It's unlikely that the riots would have made it into these pages at all had it not been for *Hellhound on His Trail*, Hampton Sides's book about the murder of Martin Luther King Jr. and the hunt for his assassin, James Earl Ray. Just as Tottenham and Hackney, just a couple of miles from my home, were being set alight, I was reading about the same thing happening in Washington, D.C., on the night of April 5, 1968, twenty-four hours after Ray shot King while he was standing on the balcony of the Lorraine Motel in Memphis. There were five hundred fires set in D.C. that night; the pilot who flew Attorney General Ramsey Clark back to the capital from Memphis thought that what he saw beneath him looked like Dresden. And here in Burton Bradstock it became impossible not to compare London in 2011 with D.C. in 1968. It wasn't an instructive or helpful comparison, of course, because it could only induce nostalgia for a time when arson seemed like the best and only way to articulate a righteous and impotent fury. And while it is true that a violent death sparked our troubles (a black man named Mark Duggan was shot and killed by police), it was not easy to see the outrage in the faces of the delirious white kids helping themselves to electronic goods and grotesquely expensive sneakers. Luckily for us, every single politician, columnist, leader-writer, talk-show host, and letters-page contributor in Britain knows why all this happened, so we should be OK.

Hellhound on His Trail is a gripping, authoritative, and depressing book about a time when, you could argue, it was much easier to talk with confidence about cause and effect. James Earl Ray, King's assassin, was a big supporter of segregationist George Wallace and his independent push for the White House; Ray also liked the look of Ian Smith's reviled apartheid regime in Rhodesia. He was eventually arrested at Heathrow as he attempted to make his way to somewhere in Africa that would let him shoot black people without all the fuss that he had caused in the U.S. Sides has little doubt that he acted alone, and indeed one of the lowering things about his book is the reminder, if one needed it, that it takes very little to kill a man; you certainly don't need the covert cooperation of the CIA or the FBI or the KKK. You just need enough money to buy a decent hunting rifle.

Of course, there are lots of people who have a vested interest in persuading us that the recent past is easier to read than the present. Paul Greengrass, the director of *Green Zone* and *United 93,* has for some time been wanting to make a film about the last days of MLK, but this year the project collapsed, apparently because the guardians of the King estate objected to depictions of King's extramarital affairs in the script. "I thought it was fiction," said Andrew Young, who was with King on the night he died. And yet King's womanizing was, according to Sides, both real and prodigious; he spent the night before he died in room 201 of the Lorraine Motel with one of his mistresses, the then senator of Kentucky, Georgia Davis. Davis has even written a book, *I Shared the Dream,* about her relationship with King. I haven't read Greengrass's script, but it looks as though Andrew Young is attempting, four decades after Memphis, to sanctify his friend in a way that can only impede understanding. Jesse Jackson, meanwhile, attempted to impede understanding there and then: he told TV interviewers that he was with King on the balcony (he wasn't), and, according to Sides, smeared his shirt with King's blood before appearing on TV chat shows. The trouble with history, it seems to me, is that there are too many people involved. The next time something historical happens, someone should thin out the cast list. Oh, and by the way, did you know that James Earl Ray was arrested in London, by detectives from Scotland Yard? Oh, yes. Your guys had done some handy groundwork, though, we'll give you that much.

It has, it must be said, been something of a gloomy reading month, not least because my brother-in-law has written another novel. *The Fear Index* is his fifth since I started writing this column, back in 2003. I have managed only three in the same period, and though I have also managed to squeeze out a screenplay for a movie, so has he. As I write, he is lying by a swimming pool in the South of France, whereas I am looking through a window at the gray North Sea. I am looking through a window (a) because if

I ventured outside I would be blown into the gray North Sea by the gale that is currently blowing and (b) because I have a column to write, and therein, I think, we find the root cause of my brother-in-law's superior output and income. "Stuff I've Been Reading" is now well over one hundred thousand words long, and if I could somehow take those words back and rearrange them into a stylish, ingenious, compelling, and intelligent contemporary thriller, then I would. But there you are. My commitment to your literary health is such that I'm prepared to let my children shiver in their little wetsuits, although I don't suppose you're the remotest bit grateful. I wish I could tell you that *The Fear Index* is a resounding failure that will lie in unsold heaps all over Europe and the U.S., but I can't. Actually, why can't I? It's my column, and there are very few other advantages to writing it, as I have very recently realized. *The Fear Index* is a resounding failure that will lie in unsold heaps all over Europe and the U.S. I'm not going to tell you what it's about. You'll only want to buy it.

I suppose it wouldn't be giving too much away to tell you that *The Fear Index* is a financial-crisis thriller, the second book about the terrifying instability of our banking system that I've read in the last couple of months. The other was John Lanchester's brilliant *I.O.U.*, in which Lanchester says that "Western liberal democracies are the best societies that have ever existed... citizens of those societies are, on aggregate, the most fortunate people who have ever lived." There isn't much downside to being the luckiest people in history, but in James Hynes's brilliant novel *Next,* which I read because the editors of this magazine gave it a prize, Hynes's protagonist, Kevin Quinn, is fiftyish and struggling—struggling, at least, with all the things there are to struggle with in prosperous contemporary America. His career has been nudged, gently and undramatically, into a backwater; he has a relationship with a younger woman he doesn't love. He spends most of his time, or most of the eight or nine hours covered in the novel, anyway, daydreaming about a couple of the standout sexual experiences of his life.

Quinn is traveling from Ann Arbor to Austin for a job interview, on a day when there have been major terrorist attacks in Europe. He's uncomfortable flying, as we all are in those periods, but this doesn't stop him mooning over the young, sexy Asian girl sitting next to him on the flight, and when he bumps into her again in Austin, he ends up killing the time before his appointment by trailing idly after her, in an aimless and unthreatening kind of a way. He gets very hot, and extremely lost, both in Austin and in his own underwhelming and regret-filled past. It's all very real and very familiar, at least to this fifty-plus male.

Hynes writes with the sort of knowing, culturally precise, motor-mouthed internal chatter that brings to mind David Gates's two monumental novels, *Jernigan* and *Preston Falls,* and I can think of no greater recommendation: Hynes and Gates populate their books with men I recognize. They're not the intimidatingly brainy and, to me, alienating creatures you find in Great American Novels by Great American Novelists. There's less rage, more doubt, more regret—and, in the case of Kevin Quinn, more of a sense that he is entirely the author of his own misfortune. His failure can't be pinned on an event, or on a scheming, ball-busting woman. Rather, it's due to too much introspection, distraction, indiscipline. Quinn hasn't worked hard enough at anything.

And *Next* takes a dizzying, heartbreaking, apocalyptic, and oddly redemptive turn. As it turns out, the atrocities are not confined to small European countries far away. As Kevin is, finally, on his way to his interview, the cab driver is listening on the radio to news of attacks much closer to home, in Minnesota, where he has a brother. The cabbie is nervous, distracted, upset; he makes frantic phone calls. Kevin, though, is oblivious to all of this. He's re-creating, in pornographic detail, a night he spent a long time ago with a girl called Lynda. "You need to pay attention, man," the cabbie tells him, devastatingly, at the end of his ride, but it's too late for Kevin.

Violent deaths take place in all three of the books described above—in fact, I can't recall a more distressing reading month. And most of the fatalities are deeply upsetting, rather than fun, although in *The Fear Index* my brother-in-law does get to bump off a sleaze-bag we don't like very much. So I needed the respite of Priscilla Gilman's *The Anti-Romantic Child,* which, though serious, contains no bloodshed, and is all the better for it. A memoir about raising a child with special needs would not have been improved by scenes of indiscriminate slaughter. (This is the sort of quality advice you'll be getting when you enroll in my online writing school, coming soon.)

As regular readers of this column may have noticed, I don't read many first-person books on this subject, despite, or almost certainly as a direct result of, being the father of a disabled child myself. There are many reasons for this, and I have a feeling I've droned through some of them before, so I'll give it a rest this time around. However, I would like to observe that it's hard to find books in this genre with ideas in them, and that's where *The Anti-Romantic Child* scores. It's not just about dealing with the tricky hand that the author has been dealt; this is also a book about literature, specifically Wordsworth and the Romantics, and how Gilman's literary heroes (she used to teach them) have both helped and hindered her understanding of what her child is and what she wanted him to be. It's smart, soulful, and involving, and it rang plenty of bells for me; I also ended up reading more Wordsworth than I have ever done in my entire life. I understand the appeal a little more than I did, but I would still argue that there is more in those poems about the natural world than is strictly necessary.

I haven't read as much in Dorset as I wanted to. Perhaps that is what happens when you invite thirty-five kids to share your holiday home with you. (I wish that number were satirical in some way, but it's not.) I have, however, discovered a new product, the

Waboba ball, which bounces off water and is completely tremendous. I'm not sure I can make a case for its literary qualities, which may mean that it has no place in this magazine. But those of us who contribute to the *Believer* have found that we have enormous influence over the manufacturers of leisure products, and that whenever we mention one we are bombarded with offers of free samples, exotic trips to Caribbean resorts, and so on. I suspect that, completely inadvertently, I have just opened myself up to all sorts of tempting but corrupting inducements. A few Waboba balls won't make up for the villa on the Côte d'Azur that this column has cost me, but the Waboba Surf, coming soon to a store near you, looks excellent. ✷

NOVEMBER/
DECEMBER 2011

BOOKS BOUGHT:
* None

BOOKS READ:
* *Charles Dickens: A Life*—
Claire Tomalin

If I were walking home down a dark alley, and I got jumped by a gang of literary hooligans who held me up against a wall and threatened me with a beating unless I told them who my favorite writer was… Well, I wouldn't tell them. I'd take the beating, rather than crudify my long and sophisticated relationship with great books in that way. The older I get, the less sense it makes, that kind of definitive answer, to this or any other question. But let's say the thugs then revealed that they knew where I lived, and made it clear that they were going to work over my children unless I gave them what they wanted. (This scenario probably sounds very unlikely to American readers, but you have to understand the violent passions that literature excites here in the U.K. After all, we more or less invented the stuff.) First, I would do a quick head count: my seven-year-old can look after himself in most situations, and I would certainly fancy his chances against people who express any kind of interest, even a violent one, in the arts. If, however, there were simply too many of them, I would eventually, and reluctantly, cough up the name of Charles Dickens.

And yet up until a couple of weeks ago, I had never read a Dickens biography. I have read a biography of Thomas Hardy, even though I haven't looked at him since I was in my teens, when I was better able to withstand the relentless misery; I have read bi-ographies of Dodie Smith and Richard Yates, even though much of their work is unfamiliar to me; I've read biographies of Lau-rie Lee and B. S. Johnson, even though I've never even opened one of their books, as far as I know. Every time, I was drawn to the biographer, rather than the subject. (The great Jonathan Coe wrote the B. S. Johnson book, for example.) Last year I devoured Sarah Bakewell's brilliant book about Montaigne, *How to Live,* even though I can hardly make it through a sentence of Montaigne's es-says without falling into a deep sleep. Expecting a biography to be good simply because you have an interest in the life it describes is exactly like expecting a novel to be good simply because it's set in Italy, or during World War II, or some other place and time you have an interest in. The only Dickens biography I have ever wanted to read until now was Peter Ackroyd's, but it is over a thousand pages long and made me wonder whether I'd be better off digging in to *Barnaby Rudge,* or *The Pickwick Papers,* or one of the other two or three novels I haven't yet got around to. In the end, inevitably, I read neither Ackroyd nor *Rudge,* a compromise I have managed to maintain effortlessly to this day.

Claire Tomalin is my favorite literary biographer; in the U.K., she's everybody's favorite literary biographer. (Everybody has one, here in lit-crazy Britain.) She's a clever, thoughtful, sympathetic critic, a formidable researcher, and she has an unerring sense of the reader's appetite and attention span. A publisher once explained to me that the First Law of Biography is that they always increase in length, because the writer has to justify the need for a new one, and demonstrate that something previously undiscovered is being brought to the Churchill/Picasso/Woolf party; and you can't leave out the old stuff, the upbringing and the education and all that, because the old stuff is, you know, The Life. But Tomalin's *Charles Dickens: A Life* is 417 pages long, without notes and index—a pretty thrilling length, given the importance of the man, his enormous output, and his complicated personal life. Top biographer + favorite novelist + under 500 pages = dream package, or so I thought. I have never once made this complaint here, but I ended up wishing it had been longer.

I am not the best person to review it for you, however, because I have no idea how it compares to the Ackroyd, nor to the Fred Kaplan, nor to the recent Michael Slater, nor to Dickens's friend Forster's three volumes. Who flogs through more than one book about the same person, apart from Bob Dylan fans? The reviewers in the posher papers will all have read the others, but out here in the real world, I'm presuming that if you've read one Dickens biography, you won't be reading another, and it's highly unlikely that you'll ever get around to any of them.

You'd be missing out, though, if you don't read Tomalin's contribution. It is a fantastic book about a working writer, in the same way, oddly enough, that the first of Peter Guralnick's two monumental volumes about Elvis was a fantastic book about a working musician. Tomalin, like Guralnick, ignores the myth and gets up close to the daily life—the walks that Dickens needed to take in order to write, the strange Victorian intensity of his male friendships, the money worries, the pro bono work, and, above all, the almost demented production of prose.

One thing is clear: Dickens wasn't thinking about posterity. In fact, I'm betting he would have said that he'd comprehensively blown his chance of a literary afterlife: he wrote too much, too quickly, to feed his family and his ego, and to please his public. He wrote *The Pickwick Papers* and *Oliver Twist* at the same time, providing 7,500-word installments of each every month; later, he then did the same with *Oliver Twist* and *Nicholas Nickleby*. He was also editing and contributing to a magazine, and he was up to his neck in dependents. (He supported his father and mother, and eventually had ten children, most of them unwanted. And his sons turned out to be as burdensome and feckless as his father had been.) He was nowhere near thirty years old.

As Tomalin makes clear, there was an artistic cost. *Nicholas Nickleby* has "a rambling, unplanned plot" and an "almost unreadable" last quarter; the plotting in *Barnaby Rudge* is "absurd," in *Martin Chuzzlewit* it is "improbable and tedious." The second half of *Dombey and Son* wastes the promise of the first with its "feeble plotting and overwriting." *Our Mutual Friend* is "sometimes tedious," and "the weakness of the plotting is a serious fault." (I re-read *Our Mutual Friend* recently, and the weakness to which Tomalin refers would have made a scriptwriter on *The Young and the Restless* blanche.) Only *David Copperfield*, *Great Expectations,* and *Bleak House* receive more or less unreserved praise, although the prissy, saintly women are always a problem, and he published *Great Expectations* with a crowd-pleasing feel-good ending. If you are feeling bad because you haven't read any Dickens and don't know where to start, Tomalin reduces your reading load by a couple of million words. The books survive because there is something of great merit on almost every page—a joke, an unforgettable description, a brilliant set-piece, a character so original and yet so perfectly descriptive of human foibles that he has entered the language—and because of the ferocious energy of just about every line he wrote. Oh, and because he was loved, and is still loved, and has always been loved. Meanwhile, *Bleak House* wasn't even reviewed in the serious magazines—they didn't bother with old tosh like that.

If Dickens were writing today, some journalist somewhere would be obliged to point out that he was living the rock-star life; there's always a slightly disapproving wistfulness to this observation when it's made about Neil Gaiman or David Sedaris or one of the other authors who routinely pack out theaters on reading tours, as if it betokens something unspeakably vulgar about our modern world. And yet Dickens got there first: it's his template, and maybe the learned thing to say is that Bono is living the successful Victorian novelist's life. Gigantic tours of the U.S., with huge and exhaustingly adoring crowds everywhere? Check. Income affected by illegal downloading? Absolutely—American publishers were not obliged to ask permission to publish the novels, nor to pay royalties for them, and Dickens spent a lot of time and energy trying to right this wrong, to general American indifference. Prurient press interest in the star's private life, combined with very unwise attempts on the part of the star to manage said interest? Both the *London Times* and the *New York Tribune* published extraordinary letters from Dickens absolving himself for the failure of his marriage. Over-hasty adaptations of the work, designed to cash in on a book's success? Dickens saw stage versions of novels that he hadn't even finished. Business relationships that fractured because of the petulant, arguably greedy behavior of the artist? Dickens fell out with publishers over advances and royalties and delivery dates with a frequency that would exhaust even the grabbiest, grubbiest contemporary agent. The glitzy international friendships? He met presidents and royalty, and he seemed to know every contemporary writer you've ever heard of. One of the most striking stories here describes Dostoyevsky calling in on Dickens at his offices in Wellington Street in Covent Garden; the Russian's consequent account of their meeting in a letter to a friend provides a profound glimpse of what we would now describe as Dickens's creative process:

There were two people in him, he told me: one who feels as he ought to feel and one who feels the opposite. From the one who feels the opposite I make my evil characters, from the one who feels as a man ought to feel I try to live my life. Only two people? I asked.*

But it was enough. Quilp and Steerforth, Uriah Heep and Madame Defarge, Fagin and Bill Sikes and scores of others... If these all came from Dickens's shadow side, then we must all be grateful that psychotherapy hadn't yet been invented. If it had, some well-meaning shrink would have got him to talk these extraordinary half-human creatures into nothingness.

I found myself thinking a lot about Dickens's formative years, and the failure of his parents to care for him properly. With no educational provision, he was free to wander the streets, mapping out London in his head, registering how short was the walk between the splendors of Regent Street and the poverty of Camden and Covent Garden. He went to see his father, whose chronic mismanagement of the family finances meant that he ended up in the Marshalsea debtors' prison, where Little Dorrit's family lived. And Charles's time at the blacking factory opened up a whole new world to him, a world in which children worked, and suffered. Pretty much all you have to do as a dad is earn some money, stay out of prison, and make sure your kid goes to school; John Dickens struck out on all three requirements, and is therefore directly responsible for some of the greatest fiction in the English language. I'm not saying that it's a good idea to piss your money away and let your eleven-year-old wander through the mean streets of your nearest big city. But if you do take your eye

---

* There are so many things in Claire Tomalin's wonderful biography I could have chosen to write about and enthuse over. But after publication, Tomalin came to the conclusion that this letter was probably a hoax, and there may not have been a meeting between the two great men. You should still read this book anyway.

off the ball, don't beat yourself up about it: the chances are that it will all turn out OK.

One of the things that did me no good at all in the formative years of my career was prescriptive advice from established writers, even though I craved it at the time. You know the sort of thing: "Write a minimum of fifteen drafts." "A good book takes five years to produce." "Learn *Ulysses* off by heart." "Make sure you can identify trees." "Read your book out loud to your cat." I cannot tell an oak from another tree, the name of which I cannot even dredge up for illustrative purposes, and yet I got by, somehow. Walk into a bookshop and you will see work by writers who produce a book every three months, writers who don't own a TV, writers with five children, writers who produce a book every twenty-five years, writers who never write sober, writers who have at least one eye on the film rights, writers who never think about money, writers who, in your opinion, can't write at all. It doesn't matter: they got the work done, and there they are, up on the shelves. They might not stay there forever: readers, now and way off into the future, make that decision. Claire Tomalin's wonderful and definitive book is, above all, about a man who got the work done, millions of words of it, and to order, despite all the distractions and calamities. And everything else, the fame, and the money, and the giant shadow that he continues to cast over just about everyone who has written since, came from that. There's nothing else about writing worth knowing, really. ✶

Nick Hornby is the author of six novels, the most recent of which is *Juliet, Naked,* and a memoir, *Fever Pitch.* He is also the author of *Songbook,* a finalist for a National Book Critics Circle Award for music criticism, and editor of the short-story collection *Speaking with the Angel.* His screenplay for *An Education* was nominated for an Academy Award. He lives in North London. His three previous collections of writing from the *Believer* magazine are *The Polysyllabic Spree, Housekeeping vs. the Dirt,* and *Shakespeare Wrote for Money.*

NICK HORNBY
HAS RETURNED TO
READING

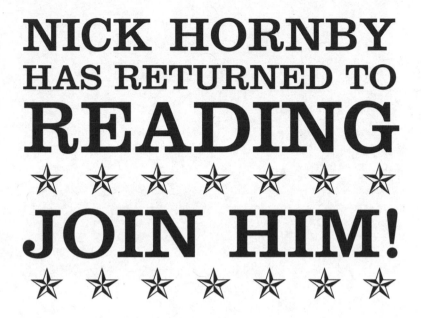

JOIN HIM!

IN ADDITION TO Nick Hornby's monthly column, every issue of the *Believer* features columns by Daniel Handler, Greil Marcus, and Jack Pendarvis, and essays from writers like Rick Moody, Michelle Tea, Paul Collins, Jonathan Lethem, and Deb Olin Unferth. Three annual special issues come with excellent bonus items, such as DVDs and the crazily popular music issue's CD compilation. Just fill out the form below for a special Hornbyphile discount!

or subscribe for no discount at all at **believermag.com/subscribe**

. . . .

Send me one year of the Believer *(nine issues) for just $40!*

Name: _____

Street address: _____

City: _____ State: _____ Zip: _____

Email: _____ Phone: _____

Credit Card #: _____

Expiration Date: _____ (Visa/MC/Discover/AmEx) CVV: _____

Make check or money orders out to the *Believer,* and mail this form to:
The Believer, 849 Valencia Street, San Francisco, CA, 94110